INTRUDER ALERT!

Roberta,
I'll never forget our
adventure to the Abalone
farm. We found trivsire some
This book is about some
of mine - it all happened,
of course changed names of course.
in Aunt Kelly to
thousands of hide
Sally
grandma

OTHER BOOKS BY
SALLY STREIB

Kids Books
Triton's Treasure: Steps to Christ for Kids

Treasures by the Sea, Volume 1
Treasures By the Sea Workbook

Summer of the Sharks, Volume 2
Summer of the Sharks Workbook

Octopus Encounter, Volume 3
Octopus Encounter DVD 1 and 2

Intruder Alert!, Volume 4

The Girl God Rescued

Adult Books

The Heart Mender

INTRUDER ALERT!

SALLY STREIB

SEAWAY
BOOKS

Sea n' See Presentations
Teaching kids of all ages to know and love their God.
www.seansee.net

Book Design by David Valentin
Cover illustration by Marcus Mashburn

Seaway Books are published by

Avid Ink Media,
a division of Big Idea Development Center, LLC
Encinitas California

Dedication

This year marks my 200th Week-of-Prayer program for kids. Jesus did not send me out alone to accomplish the mission He gave me. He surrounded me with heavenly and earthly help.

One of those helpers is Susan Cohen. Susan endears herself to me because she shares many of my sea adventures. She encourages me, listens to my ideas, and supports my book projects with schools. She shares my love for kids. Thank you, Susan! I dedicate this book to you.

Letter to the Reader

Dear Reader,

Intruder Alert! is the fourth book in the *Treasures by the Sea* series.

The story of Eric and Susan began as a serial story published in Guide Magazine under the title *The Key in the Lock*. The Guide story was so popular, the original publisher, Pacific Press, released it in book form under the title *Treasures by the Sea*.

Treasures by the Sea became a series, including *Summer of the Sharks*, *Octopus Encounter*, and *Intruder Alert!*

For many years, young readers have been captivated by the adventures of Eric and Susan. The events in this book are true as they were experienced by the author as she dived and explored the sea around Bahamas, Cayman Islands, and Laguna Beach, California. The characters in this book represent the many kids who have joined her on her many adventures.

Nature and the Bible have a powerful link. We hope you will be blessed by the adventures and lessons you discover in *Intruder Alert!*

You can learn more about Sally Streib on her website: www.seansee.net

Sincerely,
The Publisher

Table of Contents

CHAPTER 1

UNEXPECTED ADVENTURE

Eric started down the stairs toward the kitchen, then stopped, frozen in place.

"We can't let this happen," he heard Aunt Sally say into the phone. "We must find a solution before it's too late."

Something's wrong, Eric thought. He tried to catch Aunt Sally's words, but she turned away from him.

A door opened behind him. Susan, his twin, stuck her head out of her bedroom. Eric waved for her to come closer and put a finger to his lips. He could see Aunt Sally now. She sat slumped in a kitchen chair. A deep frown etched itself across her face.

"Come here," he whispered.

"What's wrong? Why are you trying to be so quiet?" Susan asked, starting toward him. She clutched a bundle of library books in her arms.

Eric crept down two more steps, then stopped. Susan crashed into him. Her books shot out of her arms and tumbled onto his head.

"Hey watch out!" Eric said, throwing his arms up. "What are all these books?" He moaned, rubbing his head.

"Just a bunch of books I'm reading," Susan said, crouching to pick them up. She shoved them into a corner of the stairway.

"Something bad is going on," whispered Eric. "I heard Aunt Sally talking on the phone. She said we needed to stop something from happening. Then she sat down in a chair and got a big frown on her face."

"What's going to happen?" Susan asked.

"How do I know," Eric said. "She didn't say."

"Oh no," Susan muttered. "I hope Uncle Merle is OK."

Susan and Eric crept down the remaining stairs and huddled on the bottom step. Susan looked at Eric, but he said nothing. She could tell that he felt worried.

They tried to listen as Aunt Sally spoke to the person on the phone for a few more minutes. Suddenly she slammed her cellphone onto the table and stared out the window at the sea. After what seemed like forever, she wiped her eyes, stood up, and paced back and forth, mumbling something the twins couldn't hear.

Susan and Eric looked at each other. Eric just shrugged. Susan felt tears trickle down her cheeks.

"I'm scared," she said, clutching Eric's arm.

Suddenly, the front door flew open and Uncle Merle stormed into the kitchen. He didn't bother to close the door or notice Susan and Eric sitting on the steps.

"Merle," Aunt Sally said. "Is it true?"

"I'm afraid so," Uncle Merle said. He gave Aunt Sally a warm hug. "They have sighted thousands of them in the Caribbean."

"Something's going wrong in the ocean and it's causing all this upset," Eric whispered to Susan. "What can it be?"

"They could actually decimate the reef," Aunt Sally said, shaking her head.

Silence filled the room. Susan looked at Eric. She knew Eric loved Aunt Sally and Uncle Merle as much as she did. They had just spent an adventurous year living with their Aunt and Uncle in the house on the beach in southern California. They had learned to SCUBA dive in the Bahamas, and they both loved the sea. Eric now had a new job with Mr. Wood at the Oceanic Institute, and Susan had finally decided to become a writer like her mother and Aunt Sally.

At school, her teacher, Miss Specks, had encouraged her to hone her writing skills.

"What does decimate mean?" Susan asked Eric, looking into the kitchen. Eric and Susan had never seen Aunt Sally cry before, or pace the floor so seriously, frowning.

"I don't know, but it sure doesn't sound good," he said.

Susan leaped up and surged into the kitchen like a wave rushing upon the shore after a storm.

"What's wrong, Aunt Sally?" she cried.

Eric followed her. "Is everything OK?" he asked, jamming his hands in his pockets and looking from Aunt Sally to Uncle Merle.

"There's an intruder in the reef and all the fish we love so much are in great danger," Aunt Sally said, her frown deepening.

"What? An intruder?" Susan blurted. "Who is it?"

"How's an intruder going to decimate the reef?" Eric asked, casting a frown at Susan.

"You don't even know what 'decimate' means," Susan said, placing her hands on her hips and staring at Eric. "What does it mean, Aunt Sally? What's wrong in the reef? Why is everyone so upset?" She burst into tears.

"Susan, Eric," Uncle Merle said. "I'm sorry. Your aunt and I are troubled, but we didn't mean to worry you. Let's all sit down and discuss this together." He motioned them into the living room.

"It's true. The coral reefs we love so much are in danger," Uncle Merle began.

"All the reefs?" Susan asked. She gazed out the window toward the crashing breakers. Nearby, the Pacific Ocean tumbled onto the sand like it had done every day since she and Eric moved to the beach house. She thought of the 100-foot-long sea kelp that jutted up from the ocean floor and trailed across the water's surface. Hundreds of fish and small sea creatures found homes and food within the kelp's giant fronds. To think that they could all die. It seemed too terrible to imagine. She sighed. The thought caused her to slump back into a chair.

"This is only a problem in the tropical coral reefs," Uncle Merle said. He noticed Susan's sad gaze out the window toward her beloved beach.

"There goes everything," Eric groaned. "I just discovered my future in photography. How can I take pictures of the sea creatures if the reefs die out?"

"If this happens, it will be a greater tragedy than you can imagine," Aunt Sally said.

"The repercussions of a dead reef system could be serious," Uncle Merle said. "It would mean the loss of untold species of fish and sea creatures. It would also be a loss of food for people of many nations and upset the balance of nature in ways we can't even imagine at this time," Uncle Merle said, looking out over the sea.

"What's causing this disaster?" Eric asked. "The sea is so big. How could one intruder do this?"

"Is it a sea monster?" Susan asked, searching Aunt Sally's face for an answer.

The phone in the kitchen rang again. Aunt Sally sprang to her feet and reached for it, but Uncle Merle was several strides ahead of her. He put his hand on her shoulder.

"Sit down, Sally. I'll get this. Everything is going to work out. Right now, we need to focus on obtaining more information." He smiled at her and winked at Susan as he picked up the phone. "Yes, Sally's here," he said.

The twins moved into the kitchen, leaning forward to hear as much of the conversation as they could. Susan liked the way Uncle Merle stayed calm and tried to reassure everyone. She felt certain he could fix almost anything.

"Mr. Wood, how are you?" Uncle Merle said. "Yes, we've heard the news and read the article in the Reader's Digest," he said, keeping his hand on Aunt Sally's shoulder.

"Yes, we all would like to help. Sally and I have talked about getting back to the Caribbean soon. We've planned some down time at Palancar reef in Cozumel, Mexico. But our plans are flexible," Uncle

Merle said.

"Mexico?" Susan whispered to Eric. "No one has said anything about going to Mexico."

"I agree, Mr. Wood, this is certainly a crisis. Email me a copy of that report right away. Sally and I will give it our immediate attention," Uncle Merle said.

"What's this about Mexico?" Eric asked when Uncle Merle put the phone down. "You just said that. . ."

"What about the crisis?" Susan interrupted. "What about the intruder?"

"Your Uncle and I were planning a research trip to Palancar reef in Mexico," Aunt Sally said, looking at Eric. "We had plans to talk with you today about it and ask if you both wanted to join us."

"But we can't go to off to Mexico. The reefs are in trouble," Susan shouted. "Has everyone forgotten about that?"

"We haven't forgotten," Uncle Merle laughed, but I don't think this reef crisis should change our current plans. It will take a week or more for Mr. Wood at the Institute to get the data together and set up a plan to help save the reefs."

"You're right, Merle. Mr. Wood can contact us at our hotel in Mexico and let us know what we can do to help. Let's go ahead with our trip to Cozumel."

"I guess that means you better drag out your dive gear, Susan," Eric said, yanking her ponytail. "And stoke up those dive light batteries."

"And what about school?" Susan asked.

"Aunt Sally has already cleared your taking time off from school with both of your teachers. You can pick up your assignments tomorrow and get them done this week before we leave," Uncle Merle said. "That way, you won't be behind when we return."

"I know this will present you with some extra work," Aunt Sally said. "But your teachers will give you credit for your work in the reef as long as you report to the class when you return. Miss Specks said she would be glad for a written report, Susan."

Eric and Susan leaped to their feet and almost flew up the stairs to their rooms. They paused at Eric's door and gave each other a high five. An unexpected adventure was about to begin, and the intruder was all but forgotten.

CHAPTER 2

A NEW FISH

"Eric, you're home from school. Good. I need some help," Uncle Merle said when Eric entered the house and dropped his schoolbooks on the floor. He entered the kitchen and sat down next to Uncle Merle at the kitchen table.

Susan joined them and watched closely from the opposite side of the table. Wires, bulbs, O rings, reflectors and batteries lay scattered all around. Uncle Merle held a small black box labeled, WATER PROOF, on one side.

"What's all this stuff?" she asked.

"Now Susan," Uncle Merle said, "Why don't you get busy with your packing. Eric and I have to figure some things out here," he said, smiling, but waving her off.

"I ordered these parts from the internet," Susan heard Uncle Merle say as she headed up the stairs toward her room. "I think we can make a powerful dive light with them."

She stopped. "A new light!" she shouted, looking down at Uncle Merle and Eric. She danced up the rest of the stairs. "I hope it's the brightest light ever made."

I'm going to be a brilliant writer like my mother, she thought. *If I read books written by the best authors out there, it will help me. The woman at the library said some of the best selling authors known today wrote these books.*

Susan looked at the books in her suitcase. One cover caught her attention. She grabbed it from the top of the pile and read the title, Murder at Ghost Hollow. She plunked down onto her bed and opened the book and began reading. She read until Aunt Sally called her down for supper, and after she finished doing the dishes, she read again until an hour past her bedtime.

The next week evaporated like dew beneath the blaze of a tropical sun. Susan and Eric spent extra time at school wrestling with the added assignments.

"It's worth it," Susan mumbled to Eric for the hundredth time as she bent over her books. "It's worth it."

Soon an enormous pile of diving and research equipment sat on the living room floor. Eric's room looked like Susan's. Neat stacks of clothes and camera gear peered from open suitcases.

"Wow," Eric said, coming into Susan's room and dropping onto the floor. "It sure takes a lot of gear just to take a few pictures."

"It takes a lot of stuff to do anything in the sea," Susan groaned.

"Why are you taking all those books?" Eric said, removing two books from Susan's suitcase. "This is a book about murder," he commented, looking straight at her.

"I'm teaching myself to write," Susan said, grabbing the books from Eric and putting them back into the suitcase. "A bestselling author wrote them. His descriptions really grab your attention. Reading them will help me learn to be a better writer."

"But you won't have time to read, especially stuff like this. We'll be diving all the time," Eric said, getting up and heading for his room.

"Writers always have time to read." Susan tossed the words after him. *I have to take time to read these,* she thought.

The week sped by as they shopped, checked their gear list and packed. Susan spent every spare minute reading Murder at Ghost Hallow.

"Susan," Eric said, coming into her room after

evening worship. "Can you help me write some captions for these shots of dolphins? You always know how to pick the best words."

"Not tonight," Susan said, not taking her eyes off her book.

"You said that last night," Eric complained. He turned and walked into his room, slamming the door.

Susan winced. She felt bad, but she couldn't stop reading. The story held her in its grip. *I want to write like this someday,* she thought. *But, of course, I don't want to write about murder and ghosts.*

Susan found that she hardly concentrated on what Uncle Merle said during their evening worship times. Her mind kept trailing off to the latest action in her book.

Friday morning soon arrived and a large, blue van picked them up at the beach house and they sped away to Los Angeles International Airport. They boarded the plane and settled in for the long, five-hour flight to Mexico. The time passed quickly for Susan. She couldn't turn the pages of her book fast enough.

Eric spent the time taking pictures of the California coastline from the airplane's window. Finally, the plane touched down in Mexico. The languid air settled over them like a morning fog as they emerged from the airplane and entered the customs office.

A NEW FISH

Susan couldn't understand a word anyone around her said. She didn't care. Soon the cool water of the reef would surround her. Beneath the sea, no one could say anything to her. She sighed, remembering the quiet places where fish cruised past and the water felt like silk on her skin.

Outside Customs, Uncle Merle hailed a Mexican cab. "The people here call them a publico," Eric informed her. The cab driver whipped the little car in and out of traffic. He jerked them to a stop at a hotel perched atop a cliff overlooking the sea.

"I can't wait to dive into the water," Susan said.

"We can't dive today," Eric reminded Susan. "We have to wait a minimum 24 hours after a flight. You know the dive rules."

They made trip after trip, toting the heavy suitcases up the steps to their rooms. "I know, but that dive law just bugs me," Susan retorted, standing in Eric's bedroom door. She dropped the last suitcase on the floor. "I'm going out to look around this place. Want to come?"

"I'll come later," Eric answered. He shoved his clothes into a dresser drawer. "I want to help Uncle Merle organize the photography equipment."

Susan slipped out the door and walked toward the back of the hotel. She looked over the balcony railing and down a ten-foot-high cliff to the ocean. Sunlight danced on the azure blue water that sat as still as glass. *The water looks wonderful,* she thought. She spotted a school of purple fish swish past just under the surface of the water. The golden sunlight flashed through their thin, frilly tails.

Without warning, Uncle Merle appeared behind her.

"I wish I could leap off this cliff and swim with those fish," Susan said, pointing to the purple school disappearing into the depths. She leaned farther over the railing.

"It looks like a great place to snorkel," he said, placing a hand on her shoulder as if to hold her back. "The water is so clear. I looked for a path or stairs going down to the water, but I couldn't find any."

"There just has to be one," Susan said. "The people who built this hotel must know that we want to get into the water."

"Even if we reach the water, we have to discover how to return to the top of the cliff when we're ready to get out," Uncle Merle said.

"That's true," Susan agreed.

"We better go help the others unpack. I'll work on this problem," Uncle Merle said, heading for the hotel lobby.

"We can't find a way to get down to the sea below our hotel," Susan grumbled, entering the kitchen. She picked up a stack of paper plates and handed them to Aunt Sally, who added them to a closet shelf already filled with food and dishes.

"You even brought paper plates in your suitcase?" Susan asked.

"We try to bring a lot of our supplies," Aunt Sally laughed. "You can't always find what you need at the local markets."

Uncle Merle came into the kitchen behind Susan. "It looks like a great place to explore the shallow sea," he said. "But I don't see how we would get in and out of the water."

"Why don't we just jump in," Susan said, looking at Uncle Merle.

Uncle Merle and Aunt Sally stared at Susan. Just then Eric joined them.

"Are you serious?" he asked, "You can't just go jumping off every cliff you see."

"Well, we must solve this problem later," Uncle Merle said. "We have to go into town for a few supplies we couldn't carry on the plane."

They dropped everything and walked down to the hotel entrance. Uncle Merle called for a publico. A beat-up looking Chevy van pulled up and a man wearing brown shorts and a red shirt jumped out. He waved a blue baseball cap at them and said a few words that Uncle Merle seemed to understand.

The narrow road followed the cliff's edge for a mile, then twisted past a small cluster of buildings and into town. The publico stopped in front of a large store with a sign in front that said, "Abarrotes, Super La Retranca."

"This is a small takeout, mom and pop store," Uncle Merle explained.

Near the door a sign in large blue letters shouted, "ICE AQUI!" Eric stopped and lifted the lid of the box and peered in.

Susan looked around. Nothing in the store looked familiar. *I can't read the words on any canned goods,* she thought. "What if I think I'm buying a can of peaches and end up with green beans," she mumbled to herself.

"I know how you could end up with some ice cream," Eric said, walking up behind her. He held up two cones, thrusting one toward her.

"Wow," Susan said, her face lighting up. "Where did you ever find that?"

"In the icebox," Eric laughed. "I don't know what flavor it is, but the shape says it's ice cream."

Susan grabbed the cone from his hand and peeled off the colorful paper. She took a bite. "Oh, that's good. It's coconut and pineapple," she said.

"I'm going to the gift store," Aunt Sally said. She handed them some strange-looking coins when she met the twins at the front counter. "I think that's enough to pay for your ice cream," she said.

Susan looked out the front door. "REGALOS EUGENIA," a sign over a store nearby read. "Regalos must mean 'gifts,'" Susan said, as they sat down on the curb and finished their ice cream.

Ten minutes later they bumped over the winding road in another publico toward the hotel.

"Look!" Susan shouted. "That's a dive shop."

Uncle Merle asked the driver to stop for a moment. He jumped out of the publico and disappeared into the shop. Five minutes later he came out, face beaming. "I made arrangements with the dive shop for some adventures this week. Everything is all set. We can get all the air tanks we need right here."

"How did you know that was a dive shop?" Eric asked Susan. "It doesn't even look like one, and you can't read Spanish. All I see is a white, round building with a pointed thatched roof, sitting on the sand."

"See that symbol painted on the side of the hut?" Susan said, pointing toward the shop. "A red flag with a diagonal white band always shows that diving is going on nearby."

"Better get your gear checked out and packed up," Aunt Sally said, as they piled out of the publico in front of the hotel. "We will dive tomorrow afternoon."

"This is a different ocean," Uncle Merle said. He handed Susan and Eric each a book. "You can't read it, but I thought you could see the names and pictures of the new fish we will see. I'll call you at

8:00 for breakfast."

The twins headed for their rooms. "Pescado, means fish," Susan called back at Eric as she entered her room. She waved her book at him. "Tomorrow I will see a new pescado."

CHAPTER 3

SUSAN'S WILD RIDE

They arrived at the dive shop late Monday afternoon and toted air tanks onto a small dive boat operated by a friendly man named Carlos. As soon as they were all on board, he cranked up the motor, and they sped away, over the sea.

"That's Palancar Reef," Carlos said, pointing at a line of foam-topped waves breaking on the far side of the shallow reef. "It's a great day for SCUBA diving."

As soon as Carlos stopped the boat and dropped anchor, Eric and Susan wiggled into their dive gear. Soon they stood perched on the back of the boat.

"Leap!" Uncle Merle shouted. Like penguins going off an iceberg, they stuck their right feet forward and plunged in. A second later, they popped up through the surface. They gave each other the diver's OK signal, making circles with their thumbs and first finger. Eric motioned for Susan to follow him down. Without waiting for Uncle Merle and Aunt Sally, they sank slowly to the bottom of the sea.

On the way down, Eric spotted the shadowy form of a shark lurking at the edge of the reef nearby. It lingered, watching them. Eric lifted his camera and pointed it at the creature hanging in the water just a few feet beyond them. He pushed the video record button, ignoring the fact that they lay in the water alone with a monster.

Then Susan spotted the shark. She reached out quickly and grabbed Eric's arm and hung on tightly. He looked over at her. Susan's face held a frown and her eyes bugged out as if at any second they would pop right out of their sockets into her mask. Eric knew she must be afraid. If only they had a steel cage to dash into and slam the door. That shark wouldn't be able to hurt them in a cage, and he could get some great shots. But now, the only thing to do was wait to see if the shark would come at them.

The shark swam to the right a little. It turned and swam to the left. It stared at them with dark eyes each time it passed. Jagged teeth framed a huge open mouth. When it paused a moment, Eric groaned. What if it turned its pectoral fins down and arched its back? That would tell him that the shark was about to attack. He knew he should decide what to do in the next few seconds, just in case.

Eric and Susan didn't see Uncle Merle and Aunt Sally anywhere. *Why don't they descend?* Eric thought. Are they having trouble with their gear? Why had he signaled for Susan to follow him down to the reef? *We should have waited for Aunt Sally and Uncle Merle,* he thought. Questions crashed around in his mind.

Suddenly the shark turned and swam away into the hazy distance. Eric gave Susan the dive sign to "ascend", and they surfaced together. Susan still held tightly to Eric's arm. They removed their fins and climbed into the boat, sinking onto a bench without saying a word.

"What are you two doing back in the boat?" Uncle Merle asked.

"What took you two so long?" Susan cried, removing her dive vest and tank. She sat on the bench, shaking.

"What's going on?" Aunt Sally asked, looking at Susan and Eric.

"This!" Eric said, pointing to the LCD screen on his camera and pushing the playback button. A close-up movie of a shark filled the screen.

"Oh," Aunt Sally said.

"I felt so small," Susan said. "I felt so helpless out

there."

"You were," Eric groaned, removing his Buoyancy Compensator Device (BCD) and drying his face with a towel.

"You have to admit," Uncle Merle said, looking at the video on Eric's camera. "This is great footage."

"Merle," Aunt Sally said. She cast him a frown, but Susan noticed a little smile in it.

"Let's take an early snack break," Uncle Merle suggested, removing his BCD that held his air tank. He placed the tank into the round brackets at the side of the boat. "If the boat lurches, we don't want that tank falling over and going off like a bomb," he said.

"Good idea," Aunt Sally agreed, placing her equipment in the tank rack next to Uncle Merle's. "We are in no hurry."

Eric and Susan removed the rest of their gear and stowed their tanks in the rack at the side of the boat. They each grabbed a sandwich from the lunch chest and sat on the bench, not saying a word. They couldn't get the prowling shark out of their minds.

"There are a lot of interesting creatures down there," Uncle Merle said, breaking the silence.

"I felt so scared. I couldn't move," Susan blurted. "I want to see the creatures who live down there, but I don't want to feel like that again."

"Susan, I can't promise that you won't be afraid

again if you go back into the sea. I can tell you about a tiny shrimp that helped shrink my fear. This is its picture," Aunt Sally said, placing an open book into Susan's hands.

"What is it?" Susan asked.

"Scientists call it the Spongicola Shrimp."

"That thing is small," Susan said. "I bet several of them would fit on the end of my finger." Susan shoved the book under Eric's nose.

"Wow," Eric said, staring at the creature. Its legs looked no thicker than human hairs. "Are you going to tell us about it?" he asked.

"She is," Uncle Merle laughed. His face lit up and his laughter filled the air around them. Susan noticed the fear begin to melt away.

"If you want to learn its secret, you must activate your imagination. It will help you visualize what you can't see," Aunt Sally said.

"Imagine that you're a baby Spongicola Shrimp, that tiny creature in my dive book. One day, your eyes pop open, and you realize that you've just been born. You take a good look at yourself. Your body is nothing more than a speck of gelatin bobbing about in a great big ocean. You wiggle the thin legs that stick out from your sides.

"You look around. You aren't floating on the surface where the sun paints the water gold. No sunbeams warm your back. You can't see the reef

31

where rainbow colored fish swish past and sea fans nod in the current. You see only the black water.

"Suddenly, a Gulper Eel, a snakelike creature with a head the size of a grapefruit, bursts out of the darkness. Its open mouth blazes with blue, yellow, white and red bioluminescent light. Terror seizes you and your heart cries out, 'Where is there a safe place for me?' You feel helpless. Fear drives you to dive as the horrible predator soars past and disappears into the darkness. The flash of light it leaves behind dims and you are alone again.

"'Dive!' a voice inside your brain screams. 'Dive deep.' You obey the voice. You twitch your little legs and drop into the darkness of the deep. You fall to one thousand feet, two thousand feet, and keep falling. At seven thousand feet, you bump into a rock at the bottom of the sea.

"The voice inside you speaks again. 'Go find the safety of the tower.' The voice sounds urgent. You spin around in a full circle, searching. You see something fastened to a rock by silver threads. You can see a tower shaped sponge that stands twelve inches high and is no bigger around than a tiny sea biscuit. It looks like a hollow, white tube of spun glass threads woven together. This is my safe place, you think.

"Your tiny heart, no bigger than the head of a pin, thumps rapidly as you swim to the tower and squeeze through an opening in the mesh walls.

"Once you are inside, a delicious sense of safety floods over you. 'I'm safe,' you say to yourself, and 'now I'm going to investigate this place.'

"You swirl around in circles until you reach the top of the tower, then turn around and plunge to the bottom.

"This is a great place, you think. There is room for me to live and grow. Soon you realize that you're hungry and wonder how to get food without going out of your safe tower. You become aware of tiny phytoplankton and zooplankton floating right through the openings in the tower. All you have to do is reach out with your miniature white claws and grab them. In a moment you are stuffing them into your mouth as fast as you can.

"Now that you are full, you think about finding a friend in your tower. You are in a safe place, but you don't want to be lonely. You glance around and dive to the very bottom of the tower to take a closer look at the silver threads that keep your house attached to the rock.

"That's when you bump into a stranger. 'Excuse me,' you say. Now you have company.

"Even with your tiny brain, you realize a truth that is bigger than you. Everything you will need is there in the tower. Your fear and loneliness begin to float away on the sea current."

"I know that this story is supposed to teach us something that will make us feel better when we leap off the end of this boat again," Eric said. "I'm not a Spongicola Shrimp. I'm a kid that has to go back into the sea without a shark cage surrounding me."

"I have good news," Aunt Sally said. "Proverbs 18:10 describes the tower that God made just for humans."

"What does the verse say?" Susan asked.

"The name of the Lord is a strong tower. The righteous run into it and are safe." Aunt Sally quoted the verse from memory.

"God is like a STRONG TOWER," Susan said. "That's amazing."

"This is one of the times when nature and the Bible talk about the same thing," Uncle Merle said.

"OK," Eric said, pacing back and forth in the boat. "I was cast at birth, into a sin-darkened world. The predator, Satan, cruises the reef of my life. He is determined to destroy me, or at least scare me to death. Fear drives me, like it did the shrimp, to search for a safe place. I cry out, 'Is there no safe place for me?' Then I spot the tower."

"Well said, Eric," Uncle Merle laughed, grabbing a hold of Eric's shoulder.

"If I were that shrimp, I'd be asking where everybody else is," Susan said. "I don't like the idea of being down there all alone."

"Our Creator longs to erase our fears. He also doesn't want us to be lonely," Aunt Sally said. "He has given us a safe place as real and beautiful as the Venus Flower Basket that stands on the bottom of the sea, waiting for the tiny Spongicola Shrimp to arrive. Our safe place is Jesus. He is like a strong tower that cannot fall."

"But how do we know God will never fail us?" Eric asked. He looked out over the sloshing sea.

"Follow His story through the pages of the Bible and see for yourself," Aunt Sally said.

"Imagine the infant, Jesus, sent to be our safe Tower, sleeping on a bed of straw. King Herod, filled with jealous rage, saw Him as easy prey. He sent soldiers to rampage through Bethlehem. Their horse's hooves kick up dust and their swords plunged through the hearts of infant boys. But God had already snatched His Son from death. He had warned Joseph, in a dream, to take his family to safety in Egypt," Aunt Sally said.

"Throughout Jesus' childhood, Satan determined to snuff out His life before He became a man," Uncle Merle said, shaking his head. "Over and over, God preserved His Son's life. Once, a maddened crowd in Nazareth pushed Him toward a cliff. God hid Jesus from their eyes and He passed through the crowd unharmed."

"There were always a bunch of priests and rulers

following him," Eric said. "They tried to get Him to say something they could use against Him. They wanted to trap Him and find an excuse to kill him. God gave Him wisdom and strength to overcome His enemies."

"I know," Susan said, wiping a tear from her eye. "Satan caused men to nail Jesus to a cross. Satan thought he had one more chance to destroy Jesus. Then Jesus would never be our Safe Tower."

"That's right, Susan," Aunt Sally said, pulling Susan up close to her. "Satan pressed close to Jesus, speaking lies that he hoped would discourage Him. He wanted Jesus to come down from the cross and leave us to our fate. But Jesus looked ahead. He saw you and Eric. He saw me and Uncle Merle. He felt our fears. He volunteered to lay down His life, a life that no one can take from Him by force," Aunt Sally said.

"Wow," Eric said.

"Whenever I begin a new day, or return to the sea, I pause and imagine myself enclosed within the safety of my own Tower," Uncle Merle said. "Then I go my way with a joy and peace I never thought possible. It's because the presence of this Tower has erased the fear and made me certain that I am never alone."

"The Spongicola Shrimp has its Venus Flower Basket," Eric said. "We have Jesus." He stood up and grabbed his SCUBA gear. "Let's try that dive now."

Uncle Merle winked at Aunt Sally. They each checked the other's gear.

"One of your octopus hoses is leaking air," Uncle Merle said, frowning. "This isn't good. It might fail to deliver air to your vest when you need it."

"OK, Merle," Aunt Sally said, "I will stay in the boat while you and the twins get that dive in. I can't trust that the small leak won't turn into a big one once I'm in the water."

"I'll stay with you, Aunt Sally," Susan said with a bit too much eagerness.

"That settles it," Uncle Merle said, squirming into his gear. Eric suited up and grabbed his camera. Together they leaped into the water and surfaced. Eric gave Uncle Merle the 'I'm OK' dive signal, and they disappeared from view, the sparkling blue sea closing over them.

The warm sun beat down upon Susan and Aunt Sally as the boat sloshed back and forth in the water.

"We're close to the shallow side of the reef," Carlos said. "You could do some snorkeling. Watch out you don't get too close to the line of breakers out there."

"Let's do it," Susan shouted, grabbing her fins and mask.

"This is a good place to wear your life belt," Aunt Sally commanded.

Susan strapped her belt in place and jumped

overboard. Gentle swells undulated over them. *Visibility is fantastic,* Susan thought. *I can see a hundred feet ahead of me.*

They snorkeled along the shore side of the reef, staying back from the area where waves smashed onto the seaward edge. Susan followed a school of tangs that darted past, flashing blue at her. She wanted to giggle, but knew water would leak into her mask if she did.

Aunt Sally swam nearby. She pointed out the retreating form of a Green Sea Turtle, waving his front fins back and forth. Without thinking, Susan darted off after it. Soon it disappeared into the hazy distance. She turned back when she realized she had entered rougher water. The boat sat less than fifty yards away, so she didn't feel worried.

Without warning, a swell grabbed her like a great giant and lifted her up. Higher and higher she rose in the water, then quickly, the swell dropped her into a deep trough. She couldn't see Aunt Sally or the boat.

Another swell grabbed her. She felt herself quickly lifted up, up, and up. She caught a glimpse of the boat and began to swim toward it, kicking her fins hard. *This is great,* Susan thought. I am on an ocean roller coaster. Up and down she rode the swells, laughing and hanging onto her snorkel.

When she fell into another trough between waves,

she saw a vast patch of Staghorn corals. Their pointed arms reached up toward her. I must get away from this area. I'll be speared on one of those sharp prongs when the swell drops me again.

The picture of the Safe Tower formed in her mind and with it came an idea. She remembered one of the rules she had learned in dive class; 'deep water is calm water.' She quickly unbuckled and removed her life belt, knowing she couldn't dive with it on. Quickly taking a deep breath, Susan dove toward the sea floor below the force of the swells. She swam as far as she could toward the boat before going back to surface to grab another breath of air. Over and over she dove, moving slowly toward the boat while in the calm water below and catching a lung full of air when on the surface. She didn't feel afraid.

When she rose up on a great mound of water, she spotted Aunt Sally swimming toward her. Carlos was inching the boat closer to the reef. *He's looking for me,* she thought.

Quickly a hand reached out and grabbed her arm. Aunt Sally had a firm hold of her, guiding her to the boat. Carlos inched the boat closer.

"You're all right. Climb in," he shouted. He dropped a small ladder over the side and helped them into the boat.

Five minutes later Susan saw Uncle Merle and Eric burst through the surface beside the boat.

"Is everything all right?" Uncle Merle said, removing his mask and spitting out his mouthpiece.

"Wow. It's rough up here," Eric said, dragging himself up the ladder and over the side of the boat.

"I got caught in some swells when I got too close to the reef," Susan said.

"She went on a wild ride," Aunt Sally said. "I had trouble finding her, even though she swam only a few feet away."

"Once again, God has been good to my two favorite girls," Uncle Merle said, laughing.

Susan noticed a bit of fear in his eyes, but he didn't say more.

Carlos revved up the boat's motor and they all headed for shore. No one spoke for long moments.

"God reminded me of the Tower," Susan said, gazing off over the sea toward the reef. "I think He gave me the idea to dive into calm water. I could look up and see you, Aunt Sally, and the boat, so I knew which way to keep swimming."

"Good thinking," Aunt Sally said. "But you had to take off your life belt to do it. I'm uncomfortable with that."

"Sally, she did what she thought was best. You know she floats like a cork. And here we are all safe and heading home," Uncle Merle soothed.

"You're right, Merle," Aunt Sally sighed. "This sea that we love certainly throws out some surprises.

One minute Susan and I swam about in silky smooth water and the next moment I saw her going up and down with the swells, out of control."

Uncle Merle reached over and drew Aunt Sally toward him. He put his arm around her shoulders and they sat in silence.

"What you say about the sea is true," Eric said. "But I don't think God can ever be surprised."

Everyone laughed. "Susan didn't panic. She turned to the Tower and found the power," Eric announced. He turned to look at Susan. She lay in a heap on the bottom of the boat sound asleep, still clutching her mask and snorkel.

CHAPTER 4

THE GIANT LEAP

The next morning Susan walked through the hotel lobby and out into the sun. A sandy area spread itself out, ending at a three-foot wall. A man, wearing a sombrero, hummed as he raked the sand smooth. Five thatched umbrellas and a dozen palm trees stood scattered about.

Each umbrella sheltered a pair of lounge chairs that faced the sea. Every few minutes a swell sloshed against the wall and shot a spray of water into the air. *It's high tide,* Susan thought, but at low tide the sea pulls back and is calm. It won't smash against the wall. That's when we can snorkel and discover what lives in that beautiful water.

The azure sea stretched out to the horizon, ending

in a deeper blue streak. Susan spotted a white cruise ship passing by. *It's sailing toward a beautiful island,* she thought. Susan sighed and headed back to her room.

"Where's Uncle Merle?" Susan asked when she saw Aunt Sally in the kitchen.

"He took a taxi into town. We decided it would be good to have our own wheels," Aunt Sally explained. At that moment Uncle Merle burst into the room.

"I got a vehicle, Sally," He said. "Come, take a look."

Susan and Eric followed Uncle Merle and Aunt Sally to the parking lot. "She's all ours," he said, pointing to a shiny, red jeep with two rows of seats and a padded roll bar. "This is UTDOO3," Uncle Merle said, reading the license plate. The twins laughed. "We can't expect the local taxi to tote us and all our gear everywhere. Besides, I thought it might be fun to do some exploring on our own," Uncle Merle explained.

"It's a beauty," Susan shouted, jumping up into the front seat.

"Didn't they have a car with air conditioning?" Eric complained. "It gets really hot around here."

"We'll get wet in the sea and let the wind blow on us," Aunt Sally said, laughing. "That's God's air conditioning."

"Actually, I did have the chance to get a car with

air conditioning, but I thought we might enjoy using the jeep with four-wheel drive. I've seen some very interesting dirt roads around here," Uncle Merle said.

"Let's get going," Susan said, jumping into the back seat.

"Slow down, Susan. You might like to know that I found out how we can snorkel along the wall," Uncle Merle said. "You were right. We can leap off the wall and snorkel along it. When I drove the jeep about a half-mile along a dirt road that hugs the cliffs, I discovered that the cliffs flatten out where a creek empties into the sea. There's a gentle current heading south that will carry us right to the creek bed. We can easily climb up to the dirt road above where Sally or I will park the jeep. We take turns driving those who snorkel back to the hotel."

"Carlos, from the dive shop, called. He's arranging for us to have a dive boat," Aunt Sally said. "It won't be ready until tomorrow afternoon."

"That's good news," Uncle Merle said. If you want to, I think we can give that snorkeling idea a try right now."

"After lunch," Aunt Sally said, looking at Eric's face. It had hunger written all over it.

"Let's go!" Susan shouted, heading for their kitchen.

They swallowed sandwiches, fruit and Aunt

Sally's raisin-oatmeal cookies, washing it all down with tropical punch.

Everyone got into their swimsuits and gathered their snorkel gear together. Susan picked up her new dive light. *Uncle Merle says we need lights every time we leap into the sea. They help us see color even during the day. I won't take the light that Uncle Merle and Eric made for me. I'll save it for the SCUBA trip tomorrow,* she thought.

"I'll drive first," Aunt Sally said. "Merle, you go ahead with the twins."

"All right," Uncle Merle said, waving goodbye. "Let's go, kids."

Soon they stood at the edge of the cliff on a narrow concrete wall. The water danced in the sunlight, but it didn't thrash about.

"Stay together," Uncle Merle instructed, "and leap on the count of three."

"One, two, three," Uncle Merle shouted. They leaped off the cliff and surfaced, hanging close together for a moment. "Follow me," he said as they jammed snorkels into their mouths and moved back twenty feet from the wall. The current carried them away.

As they glided along, they spotted a young Nurse Shark, a Green Sea Turtle, and schools of brightly colored fish they had never seen before. Soon they reached the place where the creek flowed into the sea. They straggled from the water and made their way up to the car where Aunt Sally sat waiting.

"I watched you as you came near the exit point," she said. "The current really pushed you along."

"I felt the power of the water," Eric said.

"We saw a shark, a turtle, and lots of stuff," Susan added.

"Your turn, Sally," Uncle Merle said, dropping them off at the hotel. The twins ran to the wall and Aunt Sally joined them a minute later.

"I'll count to three," Eric said. "You guys jump with me."

They leaped into the water and swirled away with the current. Susan pointed at a stingray hiding in the sand. She watched Eric chase it and take several pictures. A small school of Sargent Majors swished past them. *The current doesn't bother them at all,* Susan thought. She laughed, watching Eric hold up his camera and try to snap another picture. *Hurry, Eric,* she thought, *that current will snatch you up and whirl you away.*

Eric tried to turn and paddle back against the current in order to get a shot of a hermit crab toddling along on the sand. *He can't get enough time to focus and shoot before the current gets him,* she thought.

Suddenly Susan saw a huge orange object just beneath her. *That's a Cushion Sea Star. I saw its picture in the book Uncle Merle gave me,* she thought. She floated over the star. *It's as big as a dinner plate.* An idea popped into her head. Susan turned, facing Eric. She waved to get his attention. She put her fingers to her eyes and pointed down toward the sea floor, using the dive sign to say, 'look closer.' She watched as Eric read her signal and looked in the direction that she pointed. He had just enough time to frame the sea star in his camera lens and click off a shot as he passed over the star.

In another minute, she saw Bleeding Tooth Nerites clinging to the wall in large clusters. She gave Eric the 'look closer' dive sign as she swam by. He could focus on the shells as he slithered past them. *I'll 'see' ahead for him,* Susan thought. She felt sure that Eric had discovered that they could work as a team.

The twins worked together, signaling and shooting pictures of the sea creatures they discovered around them. They got so involved in their teamwork that they forgot about looking for the exit place.

Suddenly they spotted Aunt Sally turning to the right. She swam into shallow water, stood up, and yelled at them. She waved her arms about until Susan and Eric turned toward the creek bed and sloshed out of the sea.

"That's quite an adventure," Aunt Sally said when they walked up to meet Uncle Merle.

"I felt like a powerful swimmer," Susan laughed.

"A lot of it was that current. Let's do it again." She wiped her face with a towel that Aunt Sally handed her.

"I have an idea," Uncle Merle said as they rode back to the hotel. "Now that we've checked it out and know it's safe, I think we should try this after dark. A bunch of different creatures will be out then."

"What creatures?" Susan asked, a frown forming on her face.

"Hungry sharks," Eric teased. "We probably will see a mass of sharks tearing up some fish in a mad feeding frenzy.

Aunt Sally frowned at Eric. "I imagine the sharks, if there are any of them around, will be at the reef searching for their supper."

"You'll see a lot of different filter feeders like the Basket Sea Star. I like how it unfurls its branches while clinging to a secure coral head. It just waits until the current brings plenty of food its way," Uncle Merle said.

"And those twitching crustaceans will be out in force," Aunt Sally added.

Four hours later, they stood side-by-side on the wall. "I'll see you at the exit point," Aunt Sally said. She turned and walked toward the car.

They waited ten minutes until the golden sun sizzled on the horizon. Darkness came a few moments later. "Jump as soon as I say three," Uncle Merle instructed. "We must stay together." He counted to three and leaped into the sea, turning on his dive light. Eric and Susan stared at the dark water.

"It looks awful dark down there," Susan complained, hesitating.

Eric watched Uncle Merle surface and adjust his snorkel. "We better get going," he said to Susan. "The current will take Uncle Merle way ahead of us in a few seconds."

Susan and Eric glanced at each, and then they leaped and hit the water, sinking below the surface. Eric turned on his dive light, and a second later, Susan's popped on. Soon they burst to the surface and jammed their snorkels into their mouths. Eric clutched his camera against his chest.

The current snagged them and they moved easily along the wall, staying very close to each other. They could see Uncle Merle's light shining through the water not far ahead. Somehow it had shrunk in the darkness until it looked like a thin blob of yellow. Eric shone his light at himself so Susan could see him signal her. "Follow me," he said with his hands.

Susan shivered, although the water felt warm. The sea looked so dark. It surrounded her like a black blanket. *I wish I had brought my new light,* she thought. She groaned and cast a glance behind her, thrashing her light about. It made streaks of light in every direction. *Something is going to nip my feet,* she thought. *I don't like it out here in the dark water.*

Susan kicked her fins until her legs ached. *I've got to keep up with Eric. He's swimming like a shark darting after prey,* she thought.

Suddenly they reached Uncle Merle. Susan grabbed him by the right fin and Eric splashed up beside him. Uncle Merle almost leaped out of the water. He turned his light on them, eyes almost exploding into his mask. His snorkel fell out of his mouth. He surfaced to rearrange his gear. Eric and Susan surfaced. The three of them clustered together in the darkness, as the current carried them closer and closer to the creek bed.

"Never, ever grab me like that again," Uncle Merle shouted.

"We're sorry," Eric sputtered. "We wanted to catch up to you."

"It's so dark out here," Susan cried. She felt glad that no one could see her tears in the darkness.

"Stay with me," Uncle Merle commanded. "We'll talk later. We don't want to miss that creek bed." He pointed his light along the wall that ended in a rocky cliff, then a sandy shore.

Two minutes later Uncle Merle swerved to the right and climbed out of the water. Eric and Susan followed. They could see Aunt Sally in the headlights. She waved at them.

When they all piled into the jeep, Uncle Merle

turned to the twins. "Why didn't you leap when I did?" he asked, not smiling.

"We're sorry," Susan wailed. The water looked so dark and cold. "We only hesitated for a minute. You swirled away really fast."

"I bet you thought you were all alone in that terrible sea," Aunt Sally teased Uncle Merle.

"We're going to town," Uncle Merle said, not laughing. He turned and faced straight ahead.

"Like this?" Susan cried.

"Now?" Eric groaned. We're all soaking wet.

"Yes." Uncle Merle said, folding his arms across his chest.

"Will the dive shop be open this time of night?" Aunt Sally questioned.

"It will be open. All dive shops provide gear for night divers," Uncle Merle said.

They arrived at the dive shop ten minutes later. "Come with me," Uncle Merle commanded.

Aunt Sally and the twins looked at each other. They trailed behind Uncle Merle, Susan and Eric dripping water as they walked.

Uncle Merle banged on the door several times before a man wearing blue shorts and a shirt, with the international dive sign on it, opened the door. "What do you want?" he asked, staring at the wet people making puddles on his floor.

"We need light," Uncle Merle explained. "I want

a dive light with a strong, broad beam. In fact, we need three of them."

"You have a splendid light, Susan," Uncle Merle said. "You just didn't bring it. Always bring your best light. Bring two of them."

"Yes, sir," Susan said, looking down at her feet. She wanted to explain that she was saving the light for tomorrow's dive, but she had to admit that she should have brought it. *I can always plug it in overnight and recharge the batteries,* she thought.

Uncle Merle paid for the UK400 dive lights in four different colors. "These cost $75.00 each," Eric said to Susan. "I hope I never lose mine."

They walked to the jeep in silence.

"We bought the best dive gear we could find," Uncle Merle explained to Aunt Sally, "but we scrimped when buying our dive lights. I don't intend to be caught without a good light again, nor will I go out with others who are scared because their lights are too small."

The twins looked at each other. Aunt Sally laughed. Soon everyone laughed.

"I remember Susan's formula," Eric said as they tumbled into the car and wrapped up with towels. "A small light means big fear, but a big light means little fear."

"Fear can intrude into our lives and keep us from enjoying things," Uncle Merle said. "This is Satan's plan."

"I agree with you, Merle," Aunt Sally said. "And I have something that will help us keep fear away and our lights nearby." While you stood gazing at the latest dive lights, I got these." She handed each one a rubber lanyard.

Aunt Sally showed them how to push the loop of rubber through a plastic eye on their lights. She pulled it through and made a circle with the rubber. She pushed the rest of the lanyard through the loop and pulled it tight. A plastic clasp made it possible to tighten or loose the lanyard once I placed it around the wrist. "Even if you drop your light," Aunt Sally explained, "you won't lose it."

"So," Eric teased, "when Susan sees an octopus come up behind Aunt Sally and it's about to wrap its tentacle around her head, she can scream and throw her hands up and her light won't fly away and sink to the bottom of the sea." He threw up his hands and his light flew off to one side for a moment, but the lanyard yanked it back and it dangled at his wrist. He jerked his arm up, and the light popped right into his hand.

Susan looked at Eric. She smiled. Her twin knew a lot of stuff that helped him not to be afraid of the water.

"Perhaps we should get another one of these for Eric," Uncle Merle said. "He won't lose that camera when a barracuda nips at his fins." Everyone laughed.

"Boy, I could just drop into bed," Susan said, yawning.

"Not yet," Uncle Merle said. He stopped the car at the hotel entrance. "Wait here a minute. I'll be right back."

Uncle Merle returned in a few minutes and parked the car in their usual place near the front door. "Come on," he said. "We are all going to take that leap again. I want to erase that horrible snorkel experience from my mind forever. Nothing else will do it like a successful repeat. I've asked someone to pick us up."

The twins groaned but followed Aunt Sally and Uncle Merle through the hotel lobby and out to the seawall. "Place your hand on your mask and hold your camera against your chest when you leap," he instructed. "This time turn your lights on before you jump."

Four lights shot beams into the night sky. Susan looked at Eric. "You're surrounded by a ball of light," she said, laughing.

Uncle Merle counted to three, and they leaped together from the wall. Four beams of light fell down with them through the night sky and into the dark water. All the beams blended together, making the water ablaze with light.

They burst to the surface, adjusted their masks and jammed snorkels into their mouths. The current caught them and moved them along the wall. *All this light is beautiful,* Susan thought. No fear intruded into her heart.

They stayed close together. Aunt Sally pointed out a Caribbean Reef Octopus. It didn't seem to like the blast of light and jetted away, changing color and oozing beneath a rock. An immature Nurse Shark, on the prowl, stared at them as they swam past. Susan watched Eric snap shots as fast as he could. She stayed between Uncle Merle and Aunt Sally.

Uncle Merle is right, Susan thought. *A pleasant experience helps you forget a bad one. But what I don't want to forget is that the brighter the light, the less fear I will have.* She smiled as she spotted Uncle Merle turning to the right and straggling out of the water, his UK400 still glowing.

CHAPTER 5

THE UNEXPECTED EXPERT

Just at sunrise, Uncle Merle tossed the last of the snorkel gear into the back of the Jeep. He and Aunt Sally jumped in. "Let's go!" He shouted to the twins, who climbed onto the back seat.

"I got a call from Mr. Wood," Uncle Merle said. "His committee is doing research regarding the lionfish that has intruded into the Mexican reefs. The problem is as big as they imagined. Mr. Wood is part of a group that will gather to study the problem in a few days. He frowned and shook his head. "We just might head to Cayman soon."

"Carlos gave me directions to a dirt road that leads to a bay," he added, changing the subject. "He said we would enjoy spending the day there. Carlos knows the man who lives there. He's a serious shell expert and could give us some pointers," Uncle Merle said. "All we have to do is travel five miles south on this main road and make a left turn."

"Where will we make the left turn?" Aunt Sally asked. "I don't see a single street sign around here."

"Carlos said to turn at the dirt road with the red plaid shirt draped over a pole. It will have a straw hat with a blue band around it," Uncle Merle explained, casting a glance into the back seat. "Susan, don't let me pass that street."

"But what's the name of the street?" Susan asked.

"I guess it's the street of the red shirt and straw hat, just like I told you," Uncle Merle said, flashing a smile at the twins in the back seat.

"Merle," Aunt Sally said. "Stop teasing. We'll get lost for sure, and a low tide waits for no one."

"Keep looking," Uncle Merle called over his shoulder. "We just passed the five-mile point."

Susan stared through the window. "There's the road," Susan shouted. "I see a red shirt and a hat with a blue band hanging on a pole."

"That's it," Uncle Merle said, swerving to the left onto the narrow dirt road.

"Merle!" Aunt Sally shouted.

"It's alright, Sally," Uncle Merle said. "You'll soon see a beautiful bay before your eyes."

"Will the water be calm?" Eric asked, fully

expecting to see a bay appear any minute.

Suddenly the Jeep careened around a curve in the road, and there, spread out before them, sat a blue body of water. It shimmered in the sun and looked as smooth as a swimming pool.

"There you are," Uncle Merle said, smiling at Aunt Sally. "You'll have this bay all to yourself," he said, starting to jump out of the Jeep.

"Wait a minute, Merle. How did you know about the shirt and the hat?" Aunt Sally said, grabbing Uncle Merle's arm.

"Those are the exact directions Carlos gave me," Uncle Merle said. "When a person wants to let someone know who lives in a particular house, they just hang clothes over a pole. I suppose they choose clothes people are used to seeing them in. Whatever the reason, it sure works," he said, throwing both hands up and pointing to the bay. Uncle Merle laughed. He leaped out of the Jeep and swooped up the snorkel gear. Susan and Eric followed and Aunt Sally joined them, still shaking her head.

"Look!" Eric shouted as they neared the water's edge. "There's a tiny house over there on the beach." He pointed at a cluster of palm trees.

"¿Cómo está usted?" a voice called from the doorway of the house. Susan shaded her eyes from the glare of the tropical sun and looked back toward the spot where the voice continued to say words she didn't understand.

"It's the man Carlos told you about," Eric said. "I think he wants to talk with us."

"Look," Susan said. "I see a small thatched hut next to the house. It has a shelf at the back. I wonder what's on it?"

"Let's go see," Aunt Sally said, turning toward the house where the little man stood waving both hands and chattering away in a strange language.

"I wish I had brushed up on my Spanish before this trip," Aunt Sally said. "When we lived in Puerto Rico as missionaries, I could speak Spanish. It's been too long for me to remember much."

"Perhaps he can show us things rather than talk about them. I'm sure we could learn a thing or two from him," Uncle Merle said, putting his hand on Aunt Sally's shoulder.

"¡Hola! ¿Qué tal?" Eric said when they reached the house. The man smiled and pointed to the hut. He motioned for them to follow him.

Susan stared at Eric. "I didn't know you spoke Spanish," she whispered.

"I don't," Eric said. "That's what I hear kids at school say every time they see each other."

"Conchas," the man said, pointing to his shelf. Beautiful shells lined the narrow shelf.

A large wooden table stood against one wall. Susan's eyes got big when she saw the bottles of strange fluids, a butane burner and a machete. Stacks of pans and plastic containers sat in disarray, covering every inch of the table.

"Look at all this stuff," she said to Aunt Sally. "He must know everything about collecting and cleaning shells." She swirled around and gazed at the small shelf. Cowrie shells, pen shells, and sea stars sat propped up against the wall behind the shelf.

"Look at that," she shouted. "A Queen Conch." She reached up and ran her fingers along the glossy, pink lip of the shell. "I just have to find one of these."

"Si!" the man shouted. He pointed to the bay. "Many," he said.

"Look," Eric shouted. "The tide is really low. If we're going to find some of this stuff, we better get going."

Everyone turned and looked at the bay. "Wow!" Susan shouted. "In that shallow water it will be easy to get to those treasures."

"Muchas gracias!" Aunt Sally said, staring at the bay. She turned and ran down the beach. The others followed. "I'll help you find that Queen Conch," she said, throwing the words over her shoulder.

"And I'll get a picture," Eric said, plunking himself onto the wet sand and the edge of the water.

They wiggled into masks, snorkels and fins. One by one they walked backwards into the sea. Back and forth they snorkeled just above the smooth white sand. They covered the entire area, careful not to miss any shells that might be cruising about.

Eric hardly knew what to photograph first. He got shots of Susan turning rocks and stirring up a few brittle stars. She held one wiggly star on a finger and jammed it toward his camera. After Eric got an excellent picture, she put it on the sand, placed a rock over it and swam away.

Suddenly she spotted a large lump on the sand. She kicked her fins and zoomed forward. She grabbed the lump and turned it over. "It's a Queen Conch," she shouted into her snorkel.

Susan leaped to her feet, thrusting the shell up into the sky. "I've got one," she shouted. "I've got one! It's a beauty."

Uncle Merle and Aunt Sally stood up and looked around. They spotted Susan leaping and shouting. "I think she has found treasure," Susan heard Uncle Merle say.

"It's a Queen Conch, alright," Aunt Sally called back, thrashing through the shallow water toward her.

"Wait!" Eric screamed, standing up beside Susan and holding his camera in front of him. "Put that back down on the sand. I want to photograph the grand moment when Susan finds her first Queen Conch."

Susan lay down in the water and placed the queen

conch over on its pink lip. She let the sand that she kicked up settle. When the water cleared, she backed up and started toward the shell as she had done when she first saw it. She reached her hand out and picked up her treasure. Eric clicked away on the camera.

Everyone stood up together. Susan passed the shell around. They marveled at the wide lip and the notches where the eye stalks could stick out without being squashed as the heavy shell slithered over the sand.

"See how the lip of the shell flares out and lifts a bit at the edge," Aunt Sally explained. "A tiny Conch fish swims along, hiding beneath that lip."

"You mean to say that a fish lives with the Queen Conch," Eric asked.

"I do," Aunt Sally said, laughing. "As the shell slides along over the sand, the fish hides beneath the lip. It won't get hurt because the shell turns up enough to make room between the shell and the sand for one little fish. God designed it that way."

"How does the fish get food?" Susan asked.

"It leaves its safe hiding place under the cover of darkness of night, and returns when the sun peeks over the horizon."

"That's really cool," Eric said. "I wish I could have gotten a picture of that before Susan picked up the shell. But Susan didn't know to look for a fish because she didn't know they existed," he added, laughing.

"That's why we come to the sea," Uncle Merle said. "We learn new things every day and that provides us with many adventures."

"Susan," Aunt Sally said. "The shell has a live mollusk in it. We rarely take live shells. We try to collect specimens without creatures living in them. But I take one of each species I find in order to study them and to show them to kids who don't get the chance to go to the beach. This kind of careful collecting does not harm the habitat. You can do the same and add to your collection in this way."

"Maybe the Mexican man would take the animal out for me. He's an expert. We could get to know him better and learn something at the same time. I saw he had lots of equipment scattered over his table. I noticed a kettle and a little butane stove with two burners," Susan said.

"Let's go," they all agreed, heading up the beach to the house.

The Mexican man came out to meet them. "Que hermosa concha!" he said, looking at the big Queen Conch in Susan's hands. *What is he trying to say?* Susan thought.

Susan got an idea. *I'll use sign language to talk with him. I can tell him I want my shell cleaned out,* she thought, not waiting for Aunt Sally to ask the man to cook the shell and remove the creature.

She pointed to the small Queen Conch on the man's shelf and motioned with her fingers and her nose to communicate that his shell smelled good. She pinched her nose and pointed to her shell to say that her shell did not smell good. She handed her shell to the man. "You cook," she said, smiling.

The man took the shell in his hands and turned it over. "Este es un gran concha!"

"I think that means the shell is big." Eric said, coming up beside Susan.

Susan picked up the large pan that sat on the table nearby. She waited for the man to put her shell into the pan, but he set it on the table instead. He picked up a large hammer, raised his arm above his head and brought it down hard on Susan's shell, smashing it to pieces. Everyone screamed. He swept the pieces into a fifty-gallon metal bin that stood at the end of the table.

Susan's mouth flew open, but she couldn't speak. She watched him grab a machete and slashed the guts away from the white muscle of the mollusk. He picked them up and threw them into the trash. Susan watched them splat on top of the pieces of her broken Queen Conch. She groaned.

The man held up a large white piece of meat and said, again, "Que largo!" He turned, without saying another word, and ran toward his house. "Un momenta, por favor," he called back.

Susan dropped the pan into the sand and stared into the trashcan. Tears flowed down her cheeks. She reached into the can and picked up four pieces of shell. She held them up for Eric and the others to see. "It was so beautiful," she cried. "Now look at it."

"I'm afraid there has been a mistake," Aunt Sally stammered, trying to explain. Susan ignored her and stared at the broken shell in her hands. She reached into her pocket, pulled out a small plastic bag and dropped the pieces into it.

"Sir," Uncle Merle said when the man came out of his house whistling a lively tune. Susan knew he wanted to explain that she treasured the shell, not the meat inside it, but he didn't know enough Spanish words.

The man carried the white slab of meat on a small board in one hand and held a knife in his other. He put the little board on the table without looking up and cut the meat into pieces. He took a lime from his pocket, cut it in half, and squeezed it over the pieces of meat. Then he thrust the board toward Susan.

"No!" Susan gasped, pushing the board away. He doesn't he get it. He thinks I want to eat that horrible, dead thing. I'm a vegetarian. More tears squeezed themselves from her eyes and dropped onto the dry sand at her feet.

The man looked up from the conch meat. He saw

the tears flowing down Susan's face and the bag of shell pieces she clutched in her hand. A startled look flashed across his face. He looked at Aunt Sally and Uncle Merle. His eyes fastened on Eric, who stood beside Susan, a camera dangling from one hand.

The man groaned. Suddenly he slapped the side of his head with the palm of his hand and jabbered off a bunch of words Susan couldn't understand. He reached over and took the Queen Conch from his shelf and handed it to Susan. "You take!" he said.

Susan stood and stared at the man for a long moment. Then she took the shell in her hands. *It isn't very big and not as pretty as the one he smashed,* she thought. "Thank you," she stammered, turning away so no one could see that more tears flooded over her cheeks. She hurried back to the Jeep ahead of the others.

"We'll come again and you will find another Queen Conch," Uncle Merle soothed when they piled into the Jeep and headed back to the hotel.

"I know it isn't as pretty as the one you found," Aunt Sally said. She reached around and wiped tears from Susan's face.

"Sorry," Eric said, "but that was quite a stunning moment. Crash! That hammer came down like a whale breaching."

"It isn't funny," Susan said, frowning at Eric.

"I know. And I really am sorry," Eric said. "But

the surprise in your eyes was really something to see."

Susan thought about how she must have looked at the moment the shell shattered. She smiled. *Everyone felt as shocked as I did,* she thought. She felt a giggle trying to escape. Eric looked at her. They both burst into laughter. A moment later Uncle Merle and Aunt Sally joined them.

"I wanted to say a lot to that man," Uncle Merle said, "but I couldn't think of one Spanish word."

"He just disappeared into his house before I could get my few Spanish words together." Aunt Sally said. "I felt devastated when he smashed it. So, what did he do? He whistled."

"He was an unexpected expert at work," Uncle Merle said, shaking his head.

Uncle Merle drove the Jeep down the dusty road and turned onto the main road. A few minutes later they pulled up to the hotel. Everyone got out and grabbed their share of the wet gear and headed for the showers.

"I learned something," Susan said when she hit the stairs leading to their hotel room.

"I did too," Eric said, coming up behind her, his arms full of fins and snorkels.

"Don't hand over a treasure until you learn whether the person wants to clean it or eat it," Eric said.

"Be serious," Susan commanded, yanking a shock of blond hair that hung over Eric's forehead.

"I learned that when you don't communicate, stuff gets broken."

"Good thinking," Aunt Sally said, starting up the stairs behind the twins. "We didn't stop to get to know this man. We didn't learn any Spanish words before we came here. He didn't know what we really valued, so he gave us what he thought we wanted."

"A dead mollusk," Eric said, flipping Susan's ponytail.

After a quick shower, Susan filled the tub with water. She squeezed a bit of dish soap into the water and added her fins, mask and snorkel. She knew Eric would do the same thing.

After supper, and evening worship, it felt good to climb into bed and snuggle between clean, cool sheets. She thought about the broken shell, wincing at the thought of that hammer smashing down upon her treasure. Finally, sleep washed over her.

"Stop! Stop!" Susan shouted, thrashing about in her bed. "He's going to smash it. Someone stop him. Don't let him do it."

"What's going on in here?" Eric said, shaking Susan until she sat up in her bed.

"Make him stop!" she screamed again. When her eyes popped open, she looked right into Eric's face.

"You had a bad dream," Eric said, patting her

shoulder. "I'll go get Aunt Sally." He started for the door.

"I'm alright," Susan said, sitting up and wiping her face with a corner of her bedsheet.

"Hey look," Eric said, peering out Susan's doorway. "There's a light on in the kitchen. I can hear Aunt Sally and Uncle Merle talking."

"I wonder why they're still up," Susan said.

"Be quiet," Eric cautioned. "Maybe we can hear what they're saying."

"This changes everything," Eric and Susan heard Aunt Sally say. "We best wait to tell the twins in the morning."

"It just doesn't seem possible that something so attractive as a lionfish could become a deadly intruder," Aunt Sally sighed.

"I hope they won't be too disappointed. Susan is counting on finding another conch," Uncle Merle said.

The light in the kitchen flipped off. Susan and Eric could hear Aunt Sally and Uncle Merle come up the stairs. Susan flung herself onto her bed and Eric dashed for his room. Susan lay still, wondering what her aunt and uncle meant when they said they feared they might disappoint her. *I hope we don't have to go home early. I love every moment I spend snorkeling through warm, shallow water. I just have to discover another Queen Conch,* she thought.

She wanted to tell Aunt Sally that she hadn't meant to eavesdrop and beg them to explain their words. *What had happened? Why was everything about to change? I just have to know,* she thought, jumping out of bed.

Susan reached the door and opened it. She looked out into the hall. The house was dark and quiet. She turned and climbed back into bed. *No, I can't wake everyone up. I will just have to wait until morning,* she thought, throwing her covers over her head. Tomorrow is so far away, she groaned.

CHAPTER 6

CALL TO CAYMAN

"Wake up!" Eric shouted, shaking Susan by the shoulders. "We're going home!"

"What?" Susan said, opening her eyes, then shading them from a sunbeam that burst through her window. "I don't want to go home. Today I want to find a Queen Conch."

"Well, you won't be finding any conchs today. We're off to California after breakfast. Hurry up. Aunt Sally and Uncle Merle are waiting for you in the kitchen," he said, dashing out the door.

Susan dressed quickly and ran a brush through her hair, tying it back with a blue ribbon. A heavy feeling filled her heart. She pulled up her bedspread and grabbed a paperback book that fell to the floor.

She sighed out loud. *Maybe I will find time to read more after breakfast,* she thought.

An hour later, Susan almost tumbled down the stairs, joining her family in the kitchen. "Why's all this gear packed? Where are we going? How can I ever find a Queen Conch if we leave today? What's happening?" She blurted the questions out.

"Susan," Uncle Merle said, pulling a chair out from the table and motioning for her to sit down. "Everything is going to be all right, but our plans have changed a bit."

"We have to go home to California," Eric said, frowning at Susan. "Then we're going off to the Cayman Islands," he finished before she could start throwing out more questions. "It's all happening too fast, even for Susan," Eric laughed.

"Merle," Aunt Sally said, casting a glance at him.

"That's right, Susan. Mr. Wood has asked us all to go to Grand Cayman to help with a lionfish count, but we need to stop over in California for a quick visit to pick up some equipment and to take care of some business affairs," Uncle Merle explained. "We will leave Sunday morning, early."

"This whole lionfish thing makes me feel so awful," Susan groaned. "I know they are enemies to the reef, but they are so beautiful. Are we going there to kill them?"

"The lionfish is an invasive fish, Susan," Uncle

Merle said. "A count in different places will help scientists see how big the problem is and where it is the worst."

"We can help scientists gather information that will help them develop a plan to determine what they can do to solve this problem," Aunt Sally explained. "I think this will be a good experience that will strengthen your diving skills and an opportunity for you to make a difference."

"Mr. Woods says divers are seeing lionfish all over the Caribbean. They are reporting their sightings to an organization called REEF," Eric said. "And they've been trapping..."

"Let's say the blessing and get started on this stack of pancakes," Uncle Merle interrupted, casting Eric a frown.

"Lord," Uncle Merle prayed, "Thank you for this nutritious food. Help us make good decisions today and keep us safe as we travel. We appreciate your protection and all your help. We pray everything in the name of Jesus. Thank you."

"And help us know what to do about the lionfish," Susan whispered.

After breakfast, everyone scattered to their rooms and started packing. Three hours later they boarded a jet for California. As they flew low over the white sands of the coast, Susan stared down. She pressed her nose against the window. "I bet that's a big Queen Conch right down there," she said, poking Eric and pointing to a lump in the white sand near the shore.

"You can't see a shell from here," Eric scolded. "That's just a rock."

Susan sighed. She watched the coastline of Mexico disappear from view along with her hopes for finding treasure.

Five hours later, Susan followed Eric up the walkway to their house in Laguna Beach. She smiled. It felt good to be home. A warm California sun beamed down and a cool breeze played in the palm trees that grew in clusters beside the house. She could hear the waves crashing against the shore. "I miss the tropics already," she whispered to herself.

"We must wash all our clothing, dry them thoroughly and repack," Aunt Sally said as they rolled their suitcases into the house. "We left Mexico in quite a hurry. You brought home a lot of dampness and sea smell. Follow this list carefully and put your suitcases at the foot of the stairs when ready."

"Here we go again," Susan said, heading upstairs to her room, lugging her bags.

"Aunt Sally printed off these emails for you from our teachers," Eric said, handing Susan a sheet of paper as he passed by her room. "Looks like you still have that story to get in to Miss Specks."

"I know," Susan retorted, grabbing the paper

from Eric.

Susan picked up one of her books and threw herself onto the bed. "I'll just take a few minutes to read," she sighed, dreading to face a suitcase full of damp clothes. Soon she was deep into the plot of the story.

"Susan!" Eric called across the hall. "Help me finish this project for Mr. Wood. He wants my pictures, but I need help with some interesting captions to put with them."

When Eric got no reply from Susan, he jumped up and walked into Susan's room. "Susan, didn't you hear me call you? I'm stuck. I can't finish my project. You always come up with such good captions for my pictures."

Susan didn't answer Eric. She lay with her eyes glued to her book.

"Susan!" Eric shouted.

"What?" Susan asked, not taking her eyes from her book.

"I need your help," Eric said.

"I can't help you right now," Susan said, turning a page. "Catch me later."

Eric stared at Susan a moment, then walked away mumbling to himself.

"Eric," Aunt Sally's voice called up the stairs. "Try to get those pictures ready for Mr. Wood, so we can deliver them before we leave. And, Susan, you need to turn in a story to Miss Specks."

"OK," Susan yelled back, closing her book. She placed a piece of paper between the pages to mark her place and pushed it under the edge of her pillow. "Every time I get to a good part, I have to quit," she complained.

"I've got to do this assignment," she sighed, sitting down at her desk. She plugged in her computer and waited for it to boot up. A blank screen stared back at her. *How did the authors of the books like I am reading ever dream up their fantastic ideas. Miss Specks told me to write about what interests me and what I already know something about.* Susan thought. *The sea, that's what interests me. I'll write about the sea.*

Suddenly she remembered the Venus Tower and how excited she felt when Aunt Sally told her its story on their last dive adventure. *God created such a wonderful creature and prepared a safe place for it to live. It made me feel more love for Him,* Susan thought. *It made me think and feel different, more trusting.* The thought startled her. *Eric and I were even ready to leap back into the sea again.*

Susan tossed words onto the computer screen. She designed a sea setting to tell readers where the story took place and stopped to imagine how a tiny creature might feel sloshing about in the dark water. *This creature is so wise to obey a command in its speck of a brain and locate the safe home God places for it at the bottom of the sea,* Susan thought. *I wish I could dive down and see it for myself.*

Susan felt surprised at how fast she could come up with ideas and words as her story took shape. *I haven't had much time to think about stuff like this,* she thought. Again, she realized that she felt good when she sat and wrote about the creatures, and how each one taught her something about God and His love. *This just seems to pour out of me,* she thought. *I wonder how the person who reads my story will feel? Could it make them trust the Creator more?*

Finally, Susan stretched and jumped up. She pushed the print button on her printer. When it kicked out three pages, she picked them up, smiling, and slipped them into an envelope.

"Have you finished your assignment?" Aunt Sally said, standing in Susan's doorway.

"Yes," Susan said, handing Aunt Sally the envelope.

"Good job, Susan. I'll see that Miss Specks gets this. Here's a list of what you need to pack," she said, handing Susan a paper. "Better get started. I'm going to give Eric a list, too. If there is anything you need, let me know."

"Aunt Sally, I won't have to kill a lionfish, will I? Susan said, looking down at the floor.

"Susan, our mission is to gather information, and use it to help scientists decide how to handle the problem. I admit that I am sure they will take action to cut the number of these predator lionfish. That won't be our job, but someone must take steps to get the balance back in order to save the reef."

"I understand," Susan said. As she unloaded her suitcases, the familiar excitement of a new adventure crept over her.

Susan made a pile of clothes that needed washing, threw them into a basket and set it outside her door. "I wish we didn't have to wash everything over," she said when Aunt Sally picked up her basket.

"Susan, I've learned that going to the sea means a lot of washing," Aunt Sally laughed.

They spent most of the day repacking and chattering with each other about their new adventure.

"I can't wait to get myself into that water and see those lionfish. I do hope they fix the problem," Eric added.

The next two days passed quickly. Sunday morning, a dozen suitcases stood by the front door. Right after breakfast, a van marked 'AIRPORT SERVICE,' arrived at the door.

"This is our ride," Uncle Merle called up the stairs. He helped the driver carry the bags to the vehicle. They all piled into the van and headed for the airport, each carrying a special tote bag stuffed with valuables.

"Now I'll time to read," Susan sighed as she

wriggled into her seat on the plane an hour later. She pulled out a book from her tote bag and smiled. She glanced out her small window. *The plane is flying over tropical seas, but my mind is on solving a vicious murder case. I guess I should dream about the sea,* she thought. But her eyes slipped back to the print on the page of her book. Time sped past. She read about how a thief got captured, and a spy got lost on a dangerous mission when suddenly she heard Eric shout, "Look at that!"

Susan pried her eyes off her book and looked out the window. Grand Cayman, like a green jewel edged in white lace trim, appeared in her view. Waves crashed along the sandy shore. "Wow!" She sighed.

"See that white line that surrounds much of the island? Those are waves crashing over the reef," Eric said. "We will soon dive outside that ring of waves."

"Come on, kids," Uncle Merle said after the plane landed, and they gathered their bags.

They passed through customs. When they picked up the rental car, Uncle Merle reminded them that people drive on the left side of the road. Soon they left the small town behind and headed for the east end of the Island where Babylon Reef ringed the land just off shore.

Eric took pictures of almost everything, but Susan grabbed a book from her backpack and soon lost herself in the story's plot.

"Of course, we can't dive today, because we have to wait twenty-four hours after our air travel," Aunt Sally reminded the twins. "Don't worry, Susan," she said, looking over the back seat. "We can still do some snorkeling. Susan?"

Susan didn't comment. She concentrated on an episode of her book. *I want to be a brilliant writer like this author,* she thought. *This story has captured me.*

"You won't get her attention," Eric said. "Watch out! There's an intruder in the car." He reached out and flipped the paperback from her hand.

Uncle Merle stepped on the brakes and pulled the car off to the side of the road. "What's going on back there?" he said. "Is there something in the car?"

"No," Eric admitted. "It's just ..."

"He's talking about my book," Susan said. She frowned and reached down to pick up her paperback off the floor.

"This calls for some discussion later at supper," Aunt Sally said as Uncle Merle eased the car back onto the road. She looked hard at Susan and Eric. "But we'll soon arrive at the hotel and lots of things will need our attention."

Susan closed her book and looked out the window. She smiled when she saw small green, blue, yellow and pink houses that marched along the road. A young goat stood tied to a palm tree in front of one house, and a scrawny yellow dog lay sprawled out on the porch of another.

Uncle Merle pulled into a large hotel complex that sat very near the sparkling water. Susan stopped reading. She noticed a gazebo perched at the end of a long wooden walkway that jutted out into the water. A rock breakwater three hundred feet from land encircled the water in front of the hotel, creating a calm lagoon. Two dive boats sat bobbing in the sea next to a wooden dock.

Susan jumped from the car. "It's perfect!" she squealed.

Eric opened the door on his side of the car and dashed to Susan's side. "Wow!" he said.

"If you walk slower, you won't break a sweat," Uncle Merle teased. "That's what the islanders tell me. This tropical air is muggy and warm."

"Just right for staying wet and never drying off," Susan shouted, swirling around in circles.

An hour later, after they had unpacked, Aunt Sally called them to supper. "Look at the wonderful bowl of papayas, mangoes and bananas the hotel manager left for us," Aunt Sally said. "I made some sandwiches to go with them. Dig in."

Uncle Merle said the blessing, and Aunt Sally passed around the sandwiches.

"Sorry I swerved off the road so quick today," Uncle Merle apologized. "For a moment I thought you had an extra gecko or spider back there," he laughed. "But it looks like something else is troubling you, Eric. Do you want to talk about it?"

"Why should he bother about what I read?" Susan blurted. "I'm just trying to learn how to write by reading the best authors. Eric's mad, because I don't have a lot of free time right now."

"Susan," Aunt Sally said. "We asked to hear from Eric."

"All she does is read." Eric spouted the words. "She goes around with her nose in a book all day. You should see all the books she stuffed into her suitcase. I can't get a minute of her time to help me with pictures or do a little snorkeling, or anything else!" Eric shouted. He jumped from his seat and glared at Susan.

Susan gulped. She hadn't realized that Eric was really upset.

"What makes you say that Susan's books are like an intruder?" Aunt Sally asked.

"They are!" Eric said. "They've marched right into her life and took over."

"Susan," Uncle Merle said. "You have done a lot of extra reading lately. Are you working on an assignment or something?"

"No!" Susan blurted. "The librarian at school suggested that I study the works of several bestsellers. She said this would help me become a skilled writer. The plots in these books grab my attention. They're full of action. I can't seem to put them down," she admitted.

"Books and words are powerful things," Aunt Sally said. "I wonder if..." she began.

"Excuse me," Uncle Merle interrupted. "Someone's knocking at the door."

He jumped up and opened the front door. Susan heard conversation, but she couldn't make out the words.

"Looks like I have an important meeting with the leaders of the lionfish count group," Uncle Merle explained when he returned to the table. "I'd like to take Eric with me. We need to leave right away," he said.

"Be sure to catch Mr. Wood and let Him know I will be glad to meet with him tomorrow concerning the fish count," Aunt Sally said as Uncle Merle and Eric left the hotel room.

"I guess that leaves us to clean up the kitchen," Aunt Sally said. As they worked, the word, 'intruder', kept swirling around in Susan's mind. She frowned.

"Sounds like Eric thinks your books are like intruders?" Aunt Sally said, as if reading her mind. She turned from the sink to wipe off the table.

"I'm just trying to learn to write," Susan mumbled. *I guess I have really gotten into these books lately,* she thought. *I can't wait to read every chance I get. I want to see what happens next.*

"It sounds like you planned to learn writing skills from these authors," Aunt Sally said. "But something else is happening."

"That's true," Susan said, jumping up to gaze through the living room window at the sea. "This thing just took over."

Suddenly the phone rang. Aunt Sally grabbed her cellphone. "OK," Aunt Sally said, shaking her head. "That sounds like a good idea."

"Susan, Uncle Merle said they would be longer than he previously thought. He suggested we go out and snorkel on the far side of the lagoon. That rock wall should harbor some interesting young fish. It's a new habitat of young coral and other creatures. I think we should continue this conversation later."

"Let's go," Susan said. She headed for her room, grabbed her snorkeling gear and met Aunt Sally in the living room five minutes later.

CHAPTER 7

THE
INTRUDER

"That breakwater looks very interesting. We can easily snorkel out to it," Aunt Sally said, pointing out over the lagoon to a row of rocks piled along the half mile in front of the hotel. "It can't be over 300 yards away. The sandy sea bottom looks empty, but I bet lots of creatures live along the rocks."

"Look at that wide opening to our left. That's where boats come in and out," Susan said, jamming her fins over her dive boots.

"We should stay well away from that area," Aunt Sally instructed. "We will cross straight out and turn to the right. After we cover the length of the wall, we can turn around and come back the same way."

85

INTRUDER ALERT!

Susan kicked her fins hard and held her arms tight against her sides. She followed Aunt Sally, gliding through the clear, cool water. The sandy bottom soon dropped away, making her feel as if she were actually being lifted higher and higher. *The water always has that greyish, gloomy appearance as it gets deeper,* she thought. Soon the sea floor seemed to come back up beneath her, and sunlight easily penetrated to the sand as they neared the breakwater wall.

Aunt Sally poked her head out of the water and touched Susan on the shoulder. "You won't recognize all the fish you see. Remember that the juvenile fish that live here don't have the same color patterns as adults."

They anchored themselves in the water by plunging their hands into the sand and letting the gentle swells rock them quietly as they stared. Within moments, red, blue, and multi-colored fish darted this way and that way in front of them. A hermit crab teetered past, balancing a worn-out seashell on its back.

"A Blue Tang!" Susan mumbled through her snorkel and pointed straight ahead. Aunt Sally nodded. Of course, it's as yellow as the sun at noon right now, but it will be sky blue when it's full grown. *This really is the nursery for baby fish,* Susan thought. *It looks like such a nice, safe place for them to grow up.*

They drifted to the right, and Susan looked into

small crevices. She tried not to laugh when two crabs pranced by on pointed claws. Suddenly a small fish swam right up in front of Susan's face. It paused a moment, then just disappeared. Another little silver fish swam by slowly and it disappeared with a blink of Susan's eye. What's going on, she wondered.

Susan looked over at Aunt Sally, who jabbed her finger toward a small rock overhang off to their right. It formed a shallow cave. Just then another fish swam up and looked at them. It shone like a stray sunbeam dropped from above. Before Susan could enjoy it, the fish simply disappeared.

Susan stared. She moved closer to the place Aunt Sally was madly pointing her fingers. It was the same spot that seemed to inhale the fish. She spotted a fish the size of her hand. Brown and white striped, feathery appendages encircled its body. *What a beautiful fish,* Susan thought. Brown spots dotted every fin and even the feathery tail.

"That's strange, Susan thought, letting herself draw closer. The fish didn't dart away. It didn't even move, but just lay there in the water, still and innocent looking. The appendages and fins undulated in the gentle current. She reached her hand forward. Susan's brain screamed, stop! She drew her hand back in an instant.

Suddenly, Susan felt Aunt Sally's hand on her shoulder. They thrust their heads from the water and spit out their snorkels.

"What's wrong?" Susan muttered after spitting out her snorkel.

"That is a lionfish!" Aunt Sally said. "Don't touch it. Let's just back off a few feet, lay quietly and watch what happens."

They pushed their snorkels into their mouths and lay still.

A tiny golden fish paused near Susan's mask, as if to check her out. It fluttered, transparent fins, coming closer and closer to where the lionfish lay hidden. Susan's heart beat like the sounding off of a pistol shrimp. She wanted to scream and thrash her hands about.

"Get away!" she shouted into her snorkel. Before she could move, the lionfish jutted its mouth out, forming a funnel. Slurp! It simply sucked the little unsuspecting fish into its mouth. She watched as another and another small fish vanished into the lionfish's mouth.

Susan leaped to her feet and threw back her mask. "It's eating all the baby fish!" she shouted at Aunt Sally, flailing her arms about. "It is the intruder. It will eat every single fish."

"That's exactly what's happening all around the reef," Aunt Sally said. "Every fish must eat, but this fish is a voracious predator that destroys the young fish that would normally replenish the reef."

THE INTRUDER

"Eric called it an ambush predator. He's right. I saw that for myself," Susan wailed. "It just lays there sucking up the clueless fish as they swish past."

"We need to bring Eric and his camera here as soon as he returns." Susan said, throwing herself back into the water and heading toward shore. Aunt Sally followed, kicking her fins hard to keep up with Susan. They both straggled out of the water and headed for the hotel room as fast as they could. When they opened the door, they saw Uncle Merle and Eric sitting in the kitchen.

"Lionfish are intruders. They're killers!" Eric shouted, leaping to his feet, the minute Aunt Sally and Susan came through the door.

"They aren't part of the native habitat, and they don't have any natural enemies. That's why it's such an enormous problem. They just keep on reproducing. They'll eat almost anything, killing off young fish that will never grow up to live in the nearby reef. Some guy gutted a lionfish he caught and found nineteen small fish inside. Can you believe, nineteen! There was even a dead baby octopus and a cleaner fish in its stomach. These guys are like vacuum cleaners. Slurp! You're gone!" Eric shouted the words at the two standing in the doorway, dripping water into small pools around their feet.

"Eric isn't telling the half of it," Uncle Merle interrupted, moving toward the front door. "These lionfish can reduce the marine creatures in an area by 80 to 90% in only five weeks."

"They eat up all the fish around them. That's the problem," Eric said, waving his hands. "These gluttons can go without food for up to 3 months until they find a new place to feed."

"Sally, this invasive lionfish is out-breeding, out-living and out-competing every other native fish out there. Scientists are talking about complete destruction of the reef system because of loss of fish stocks," Uncle Merle said, shaking his head.

"Lionfish aren't aggressive to humans, but you can get stung by one of their spines. They are like little loaded guns," Eric said. "And they have thirteen big spines on their backs."

"Not that a lionfish is bad. It's that they have no predator fish to keep them in check, so they just intrude and destroy without restraint in areas not meant to have them present," Uncle Merle explained.

"It would be a terrible sight to watch them suck up those little fish, and even crabs," Eric said, shaking his head.

"We know. We saw them," Susan said, throwing her snorkel gear onto the floor. "We saw them," she repeated the words, shaking her head.

"Sorry," Uncle Merle said. He handed them each a dry towel from the kitchen table. "I didn't realize you were soaking wet."

"You saw them?" Eric shouted the words. "You just saw a lionfish?"

"We saw them right out at the far edge of the lagoon," Susan said, staring at Eric.

"We snorkeled out to the rock breakwater that protects the lagoon. The rocks provide hiding places for lots of creatures," Aunt Sally said, drying off. "We watched those lay-in-wait predator lionfish gulp down a dozen small fish. Finally, we couldn't take it anymore and headed in to get you guys."

"It's terrible," Susan said, dropping into a kitchen chair. The others joined her.

"You actually watched those predators hunt?" Eric asked again.

"I swam that close to two of them," Susan said, holding up her hands and spreading them two feet apart. "You should have seen how the lionfish's mouth puckered up. It formed a round tube that stretched forward, almost popping off the end of its face," Susan said, her eyes opening big. She leaned right into Eric's face. "Slurp!" she shouted. "In went the victim. It never knew what hit it."

Eric jerked his head back and jumped up. "Wow!" he said.

"That's true," Aunt Sally agreed. "It was not a pleasant experience."

"You girls didn't have your camera along, did you?" Uncle Merle questioned. A hopeful look formed on his face, then fell right off when Aunt Sally and Susan both shook their heads.

"It sounds like you learned a lot at the meeting," Aunt Sally said.

"We did," Uncle Merle said. "One thing that will interest you is that you don't have to worry about being attacked by these fish. They don't bother humans and . . ."

"It's a good idea to stay clear of those fins," Eric interrupted. "If you don't like the idea of a lot of pain and swelling, shortness of breath, allergic reactions and even seeing some of your body parts paralyzed."

"Eric!" Uncle Merle said, casting Eric a stern look.

"Of course, the whole thing doesn't last longer than 24 hours. It gradually goes away," he added, brightening.

"Mr. Wood gave instructions to groups of divers who plan to take a count. I imagine that, later, other divers will net the intruders and remove them from the reef in as many places as possible. He laid out several papers on the table. Let me explain," he said. Susan, Eric, and Aunt Sally huddled around him. "This is what we can do to help," he said.

"Divers around the world are actually competing to see how many of these fish they can capture," Eric whispered to Susan.

"That would be easy. Lionfish don't dart away when

approached," Susan said. "They just lay there."

"Our part right now will be to study the situation around the three Cayman Islands. After we, and other divers complete the study, we will decide on a strategy." Uncle Merle continued.

"I can't believe something so beautiful could be such a big problem," Susan said.

"That is difficult to believe," Aunt Sally said, shaking her head. "But we saw that intruder with our own eyes today."

"What exactly is an intruder?" Sally asked, looking at Uncle Merle.

"I believe it is anything that works its way in and takes over, injuring and even destroying."

Works its way in and takes over, Susan thought. *It might even be attractive or appear desirable.*

"Listen," Aunt Sally said. "I have a suggestion. Eric looks like he is about to burst if he doesn't get that camera going, and we don't have to be at the reef until tomorrow morning. Why don't we all go out to the breakwater and get a look at the little monsters?"

"Yes!" Eric said, heading for his bedroom. "Susan, I'll need your help," he said, bounding up the stairs and past her room.

Aunt Sally and Uncle Merle laughed. They gathered their snorkel equipment and soon stood by the front door. "Come on!" Sally said, heading down the stairs and grabbing her still wet gear bag.

The afternoon sun beamed onto them, and a breeze cooled the air. They waded right into the clear water. Aunt Sally gave them a snorkel plan.

"Go out a bit to the right and when you reach the breakwater, turn right and follow it along. I'll team up with Uncle Merle, and Susan and Eric will work as a team. Don't be in a hurry. Stay still and watch."

"Shouldn't we stop at any spot reefs that might be near the breakwater? Susan asked. "I know that small fish and lionfish haunt these areas."

"Good idea, Susan. The water is so shallow and clear. I'll get some great shots," Eric said.

"Remember one thing," Uncle Merle said. "No touching!"

"Don't worry," Eric and Susan said as they placed their masks onto their faces and jammed the snorkels into their mouths.

As soon as they passed the deepest area of the lagoon, they saw the breakwater in the distance. Sunlight streamed down, its golden fingers sent patterns of light and dark that danced above the sand and over their swimsuits.

When they reached the breakwater, everyone stopped and stared at the rocks that formed the many overhangs and small caves. Susan moved ahead of Eric and stopped. She gave a sign for him to come close. He inched his way up to her, looking at the exact spot where she pointed. A big smile spread itself over his face He lifted his camera and clicked away. Tiny fish moved close, twitching transparent fins. They disappeared. Eric stood up, almost leaping from the water. Susan joined him.

"This is the most terrible, fantastic thing I've ever seen in the sea," he shouted. "Look!" he said, turning toward Aunt Sally and Uncle Merle, then splashing down into the shallow water. He kicked his fins and torpedoed toward a small spot reef just back from the breakwater. The others joined him.

There in the white sand near the miniature reef, lay two sea urchins with long, black spines. Dozens of tiny fish swam in between the spines. Four lionfish lay close by.

I hope Eric gets his shots, Susan thought. He pointed at the sea urchins and signaled Aunt Sally and Uncle Merle to come close. Susan smiled at him. He looked about to burst.

Three of the lionfish banded together, and the fourth one swam around to the far side of the urchins. Susan almost held her breath, waiting to see what might happen.

The lone lionfish fluttered its fringed spines, poking them into the area around the sea urchin spines. Susan wanted to scream and dance about in her excitement, but all she could do was lay there and wait. Aunt Sally gave her the dive sign that meant,

'Stay still.'

A second passed. It seemed like forever. Suddenly, the tiny fish turned and fled in the opposite direction to get away from the fluttering enemy. They darted right into the waiting mouths of the other three lionfish. Sally gasped. She saw Eric clicking away.

"This can't be real," Eric said, leaping to his feet. "Fish hunting like a pack of wolves. Did you see that?" Eric called out when Susan stood up.

"I saw it," Susan said.

"We did, too," Aunt Sally and Uncle Merle shouted together, removing their masks. "Absolutely amazing!" Aunt Sally said.

"Double check to see what you got on the camera," Uncle Merle said. "This is such shallow water and the lighting should be perfect. I hope you recorded that behavior. We will take your pictures to the committee for viewing."

"Let's get back to the room," Aunt Sally said. "I have some calls to make."

They snorkeled back to shore, stopping at several small spot reefs, but saw no more lionfish hunting.

"An intruder moves in and takes over." Susan repeated the words that Uncle Merle used to explain the action of a lionfish, the enemy intruder. *Could her books act like intruders? She did have trouble getting rid of some pictures the writers had painted with their words. They stuck in her mind. They have also taken over my time lately,* she thought.

Susan watched as Eric dropped his gear into the wash tank and headed up to his room. Soon she saw the computer screen blink on. She paused by his door and watched as he pulled his chair closer to the desk and brought up his pictures.

"Eric," Susan said, "I'd like to help you with your captions after breakfast tomorrow. Aunt Sally and Uncle Merle have an early meeting."

"Thanks, Susan," Eric said. "That would be great."

What do I do now, thought Susan, *if reading novels isn't the best way for me to learn to write because it intrudes into my life and takes control, how will I learn? I want to get rid of those awful pictures that reading these books put into my mind. I want to become a skilled writer.*

"Good night, Susan," Aunt Sally said, pausing at her door. "It's been quite a day."

"I know scientists say they have to kill all the lionfish," Susan groaned. "I just wish there was something they could do. I had no idea that something that looked so beautiful could be such an enemy," Susan continued. "Can other things that look so good become an enemy?"

"What do you think?" Aunt Sally said, sitting on the edge of her bed.

"I don't know," Sally said. "I think it can happen

even if you don't expect it. I only meant to read so I could learn how excellent authors get people to keep buying their books. They need to have excellent writing skills. I never planned to write about ghosts and murder. Once I started reading the books, I couldn't stop. I didn't want to stop."

"Sounds like you've done some serious thinking. Watching those little unsuspecting fish get sucked up by the predator shocked me, too." Aunt Sally said, reaching out and pulling the sheet up around Susan's chin.

"I didn't expect my novel reading to cause so much trouble," Susan moaned. "I still want to write and do it well. There must be a better way."

"I understand," Aunt Sally said, kissing Susan on the cheek. "I have a good plan that will help you reach your goal. Let's talk about it tomorrow. Good night, now."

A good plan, Susan thought. She liked the idea. Before she could think about anything else, she yawned and fell asleep.

CHAPTER 8

STINGRAY CITY SURPRISE

"Sally," Uncle Merle said when he came into the kitchen the next morning. "I want to take Eric with me when our group gathers to mark off special areas for the lionfish count. He can record our work with his camera. This will help other groups who will dive in reefs around the world."

"Good idea, Merle," Aunt Sally laughed. "Susan and I have a plan of our own. I'll be ready to do that deep dive when you return this afternoon. We don't expect that the deeper reef will reveal any more lionfish infestation than the shallow reef, but we want to check it out," Aunt Sally said.

Eric tumbled down the stairs into the kitchen. He grabbed a pancake and stuffed it into his mouth.

"Would you like to join the committee this afternoon, Eric?" Uncle Merle asked.

"Sure," Eric said. "I'd like that."

"Great," Uncle Merle said, piling his own plate high with Aunt Sally's pancakes. In the next few minutes everyone ate the last of the pancakes. Uncle Merle and Eric gathered their cameras and gear and headed out the front door. Susan waved as they drove away. *I wonder what the plan is that Aunt Sally has in mind for us,* she thought.

"What about your plan?" Susan said as they had cleared the table and put the dishes into the dishwasher.

"You have already discovered that you want to be a writer," Aunt Sally said, smiling. "You've realized that studying the skills that excellent authors use is important. I think you are on the right track."

"But something's wrong," Susan said, frowning. "it has excited me to read the stories. However, afterwards I don't feel good about it, and I don't think I'm learning what I really wanted to learn."

"These novelists seem to have captured your attention," Aunt Sally said.

"I'm captured all right," Susan sighed. "I can't wait to read the next book in the series and see what will happen."

"So, you would say that what you have read has…" Aunt Sally started.

"It's become a habit. Eric says calls it an intruder. Uncle Merle says an intruder is something that comes in and takes over," Susan said, wiping away tears from her eyes. "All I think about is reading the next book to find out what happens. And ugly thoughts and pictures keep popping up into my mind. I even have nightmares about some stories."

"All right," Aunt Sally soothed, moving close to Susan and offering her a tissue. "I know that you remember that God has given you a gift that you can use to help others learn more about Him. You also know that Satan wants you to use your gift for just the opposite. That is why he has intruded into your life. I think I have a plan to help you reach your goal without the intruder barging in. It ought to put a smile on your face."

"That sounds great," Susan admitted, wiping her eyes. "What's your plan?"

"The first part of my plan is to help you have an experience that will satisfy and excite you. It will also help you discover the plan that God has established for those who want to choose the best materials to read and write about."

"What kind of experience are you talking about?" Susan asked, her eyes lighting up with interest.

"When Eric comes back for lunch," Aunt Sally said, "I'm sending you two off on a visit to the city. When you return, we can talk about your experience.

I think it will help you develop a plan to become a talented writer," she laughed.

"The city?" Susan asked. "I can't imagine what I can learn about writing in a city."

"Oh, I better get ready for that dive with Uncle Merle this afternoon," Aunt Sally said, casting a glance at the kitchen clock. "Time has gotten away from us."

Susan watched Aunt Sally gather her dive gear from the veranda. She bounded up the stairs to her room. Instead of taking a novel from her suitcase, she grabbed her fish identification guide instead. *I'll make a list of the fish I have already seen and look them up on the computer to learn as much as I can about each one,* she thought.

Two hours later, Eric walked in through the front door. Susan heard him and almost flew down the stairs. "You're home," she said.

"We marked off several areas and volunteer divers counted the lionfish in each spot," Eric said, dropping wet gear on the floor. "I'm hungry."

"Looks like you had a good morning," Aunt Sally said, coming downstairs and into the kitchen. She laughed at Eric's tousled hair.

"There are lots of divers going to work as we speak," Uncle Merle said, joining them in the kitchen and dropping into a chair.

"I'll serve lunch as soon as you two dry off," Aunt

Sally said. She pulled plates out of the kitchen cupboard and placed silverware on the table.

"We're going to the city," Susan blurted, when they had gathered around the table. "It's part of a plan."

Eric looked around him. "I don't have time to go to the city today," he objected. "There is a lot to do out there at the reef."

Aunt Sally smiled and cast a glance at Uncle Merle. "Did you call Pastor McDonald?" she asked.

"I did," Uncle Merle said, smiling. "He was happy to consent to our plan, and will be here within the hour. While the twins visit the city, we can take that deep dive."

"The city," Eric groaned, after he finished his third sandwich. He left the table and headed for his room.

"Be sure to put a new battery in your camera," Uncle Merle called up the stairway. "You took a lot of shots out there today. It might be a good idea to take some snorkel gear along," he added. "You might have time to get into the water on the way home."

"I'm sending you off with a snack," Aunt Sally said when Pastor McDonald arrived, and Susan and Eric followed him to his car.

"Pastor McDonald!" Susan said. "It is good to see you again."

"Great to see you," Pastor McDonald said, placing

his hand on Eric's shoulder. "You must have grown a foot taller since you last visited us here on Cayman."

"Off with you guys," Uncle Merle said. "Have fun."

Susan and Eric waved goodbye and slid into the car seats. "I hope we won't be long in the city," Eric said. "I have to get back and help at the reef."

"I hear your project at the reef is going well," Pastor McDonald said. "But there is something you need to see at the city. Your aunt and uncle thought it would interest you while they dive the wall."

"We will drive along the north edge of Grand Cayman," Pastor McDonald explained. "I can park the car at Rum Point and we will take a boat to the city."

"Where's this city?" Eric said, staring out the window. "I didn't think a small island like Cayman had enough people to make a city."

"It does," Pastor McDonald teased.

Susan peered out the car window. A great expanse of shallow, turquoise water spread out before her. She saw a line of white far from shore, then darker water that looked deep, and ended at the horizon in a band of very deep blue. She did not see a city.

"We have arrived," Pastor McDonald said, bringing the car to a stop beneath a pine tree with a thin trunk and very long needles.

"That's the boat we will take," Pastor McDonald

said. He pointed toward a twenty-five-foot boat bobbing on the sea just off the dock. Eric read, *Wave Runner*, printed in large red letters on the bow.

Eric grabbed his snorkel gear and his camera. "This is getting interesting. I've never gone to the city in a boat."

Pastor McDonald started up the engines. He released the ropes that held the boat to the dock. *Wave Runner* sprang forward like a dolphin leaping across the sea.

"Where is the city?" Eric asked, but no one answered. The boat skimmed over the sea and set Eric's hair flying. He looked at Susan. Her ponytail stood straight out and a smile covered her face. Her eyes danced, and she flung her arms out as if trying to catch the wind.

Soon Pastor McDonald slowed *Wave Runner*, and they eased up near a group of boats that faced land. He threw out the anchor and shut off the motor.

"OK, kids," Pastor McDonald said. "This is Stingray City. Get into your snorkel gear and sit down on the back of the boat for a moment. I want to give you some instructions."

"Stingray City," the twins chorused together.

"Yes," Pastor McDonald laughed. "This is an actual city."

Susan and Eric geared up and sat perched on the back of the boat. Susan could hear groups of people laughing and splashing in the water. She saw dark shadows in the water moving up to the groups and swirling past them.

"The creatures you see gliding past are Southern Stingrays. They won't harm you. There is a safe way to hold them if you choose to."

"A whole city of sea creatures," Susan said, turning to stare at the shallow water that surrounded the boat. Dark shadows of the rays passed close by and she could see their triangular backs and long, pointed tails. They swam right and left, close together, but didn't bump into each other.

Eric stared at the water. "This really is a city," he said. "Time for pictures." He clung to his camera and looked as if he would jump out of his skin if someone didn't let him get into the water soon.

"Wait, a minute. You need to know a few things that will help you enjoy your adventure," Pastor McDonald said. "You should approach the ray at the snout end, not the tail. Stick your arms out, palms up. The ray will come right up to you. It will rest on your extended arms. Your arms will be on both sides of the ray's body, beside the gill slits on its underside."

"What will the skin feel like?" Susan asked, frowning.

"A lot like wet rubber," Pastor McDonald said.

"Where's the mouth," Susan asked. "I like to know

where the mouth is."

"She also likes to know how big it is, too," Eric said, flipping Susan's ponytail.

"You're the one who got a relieved look on your face when Uncle Merle told you that a Blue Whale can open its mouth and take you in, but can't swallow you because its throat is too small. It would probably just spit you out."

"Size does matter here, too," Pastor McDonald said, laughing. "The male rays are usually smaller than the females. The young rays, that are even smaller, are more active than the adults. They dart off here and there. You will find the larger rays easier to hold on to."

"Where did you say their mouth is?" Susan persisted. She made a face at Eric, but he was too busy adjusting his camera to notice.

"Susan, the mouth of a Southern Stingray is on the ventral or underside, in front of the gill slits behind the snout. Don't be afraid. These rays won't bite you. Just don't lift them entirely out of the water when you put your arms underneath them."

"Let's go," Eric said, swinging his legs over the side of the boat and plunging into the water. Susan followed. The cool, crystal clear sea enveloped her. Soon she stood ten feet from the boat in waist deep water. She could see the rays swirling past and turning to come by again. A large ray approached her.

"Stick your arms out," Eric shouted. "I'll dive down and get your picture."

Susan stifled an urge to giggle. She thrust her arms out, and the ray moved right up to her. It rested on top of her outstretched arms. "The ray's skin is as smooth as silk! Susan shouted, trying to stand still. "Wow. I'm holding a real stingray."

"You can give the ray a kiss on its wings," Pastor McDonald saidwith a laugh. "Everyone does it. And, the rays will stay out of your way and just glide around you, if you stand quietly."

"You've probably noticed that she does nothing quietly," Eric said when he burst up through the surface after taking several shots of Susan holding the ray. "I always thought rays were solitary creatures," Eric said, moving to the side of the boat. "But there are dozens around here, congregating together."

"That's right, Eric. However, these rays have been adapting to this special situation. They know that boats full of hundreds of people will come at the same time each day. They have learned that there will be plenty of squid and ballyhoo offered to them. So, they adjust to feeding during the day and sleeping at night. Under normal conditions, wild rays will have the opposite behavior. Scientists are studying this behavior change and how it affects the animals."

"How many of them come to the sandbar to feed like this?" Eric said. "It's a big sandbar."

"Up to a hundred come at one time, Eric." Pastor McDonald said. "The sandbar extends for over thirty-five square miles. Can you see the white line beyond the sandbar?"

"That must be a reef. It looks like it arches right across the mouth of the North Sound," Eric said.

"That is exactly what it does," Pastor McDonald said. "It makes this protected lagoon possible."

"Take some shots of me," Eric said, handing Susan the camera.

Susan watched Eric extend his hands beneath a small ray. She took a picture of his face lighting up. "I can't believe that I'm holding this thing," he said.

Susan dove under the surface and got some pictures of Eric interacting with several rays as they swam up to him. She heard Pastor McDonald laughing. He handed Eric a net bag that contained pieces of squid and ballyhoo. Eric reached out and offered a piece of fish to a young ray that swam past. Soon a dozen rays came near.

"They're lining up for the free handouts," he shouted to Susan.

When Eric emptied the bag, he snorkeled over to the boat and handed it to Pastor McDonald. "What do stingrays normally eat?" he asked.

"Southern Stingrays eat clams, crustaceans and

other bivalves," He explained. "They're bottom feeders, so they can easily find these creatures."

"Speaking of feeding," Eric said. "I'm hungry. What did Aunt Sally send in that ice chest?"

"Come aboard and dry off," Pastor McDonald said, handing them each a towel. "I promised your Aunt Sally I'd have you back by 4:00 or 5:00 o'clock this afternoon."

Susan and Eric climbed aboard and wrapped up in dry towels.

"That's one cool city," Eric said. He opened the ice chest and pulled out a cold drink and some of Aunt Sally's cookies.

Pastor McDonald started the motors, and they sped over the glassy sea toward Rum Point. All the way back to the hotel, the twins questioned Pastor McDonald about the life habits of the stingrays.

"That's a spectacular city!" Susan blurted the minute they said goodbye to Pastor McDonald and entered the kitchen where Aunt Sally stood preparing supper. She turned and headed up the stairs. *I can't wait to get into a hot shower,* she thought.

"Supper," Uncle Merle called up the stairs an hour later. Aunt Sally and the twins joined Uncle Merle in the kitchen.

"Our dive went well," Uncle Merle said. The family placed the dirty dishes into the sink and gathered in the living room for evening worship.

"We decided that shallow water suits the lionfish," Uncle Merle said. "But the worship topic for tonight is about your visit to Stingray City. God created your minds, and He knows how you learn best.

"Susan, what do you think happened to you during the very first part of your adventure?" Aunt Sally questioned.

"I can tell you what happened to me," Eric said, not waiting for Susan to answer. "Those rays got my attention. When I heard we had to go to the city, I didn't want to go. I had my mind on other stuff before that."

"What do you think, Susan?" Aunt Sally asked.

"I agree with Eric. Once I saw the rays, I didn't think about anything else. The time just evaporated like morning mist under the tropical sun," Susan said. "Those rays had my complete attention. I wanted to know everything about them."

"You have just discovered the first miracle God uses when He wants to teach someone something or help them discover truth. He has to . . ."

"To get their attention," Eric finished. "That's not always easy."

"You are exactly right, Eric."

Aunt Sally picked up a blank piece of paper and wrote:

1. Nature grabs your attention and captures your curiosity.

"Why do you think that is so important?" Uncle Merle asked.

"I don't think a person can learn anything until the teacher has his attention," Eric said.

"Those rays had his attention," Susan said. "The only reason he came out of the water was because he got hungry."

They talked about stingrays and the joys of touching beautiful creatures that God created. Susan felt certain she would dream all night, about creatures slithering past like eagles soaring above in unseen air currents.

"These knobby heads learn fast," Uncle Merle said, using his affectionate name for them. "I'd like to have a prayer for right now, as we end our evening worship."

Everyone bowed their heads, and Uncle Merle prayed. "Dear God, we thank you for keeping us safe today. You really grabbed Susan's and Eric's attention today. You showed them how you can use nature to reach out and draw them in close to you. Thank you for creating those beautiful rays. We know you love us very much. We pray this in Jesus' name. Amen."

"We will talk more tomorrow." Aunt Sally said, smiling. "I know two young people who could use some sleep."

"Goodnight," the twins called out as they climbed

the stairs to their bedrooms.

"Number one," Eric heard Susan whisper as she entered her room, and leaped into bed.

"Nature captures your attention," Eric called out as he paused at her open door. Susan didn't move. She had already fallen asleep.

What number two is, Eric wondered, crawling between two crisp, cool sheets. But before he could think about it anymore, he fell asleep.

CHAPTER 9

DISCOVERY

A seagull swooped past Susan's window and squawked. The racket awakened her and she sat up. She reached out and grabbed the paperback that sat on her bedside table. Ah! She sighed, opening the book to the page that held a blue bookmark.

"Wait!" she said, slamming the book shut. *I don't want this book to have my attention. I'm on a tropical island. I want to think about stingrays and the sea. I want to learn everything I can about everything around here. These books have had my attention far too long,* she thought.

Susan jumped out of bed. She gathered the paperback books scattered about the room and shoved them into a plastic bag. She tied the bag shut and dropped it into her empty suitcase. *I can't throw them away,* she thought. *I have to return them to the library.*

Suddenly she felt a strange emptiness. She realized how much she had looked forward to reading the books. What could she do to keep herself busy? *I know*, she thought. She wiggled into a pair of yellow shorts and a shirt with pictures of tropical fish on it.

"Eric," she called, knocking on his door. "Wake up."

"I'm awake," he said. "I was just struggling with some computer stuff."

"I'd be glad to help you with some captions for your pictures," Susan said.

"You would?" Eric questioned, staring at her. He jumped up from the computer. "Take my chair," he said, grabbing another and pulling it up beside Susan, who stared at the screen. "You should see the ones we took at Stingray City."

Soon the twins started laughing at the pictures, and they each made suggestions about which ones to save or delete. *Eric sure knows how to improve the composition and colors of the shots,* Susan thought. She added interesting captions beneath each picture. They forgot about breakfast until Aunt Sally called them.

"Anyone up there hungry," She asked. "We have to meet the others at the reef in two hours."

INTRUDER ALERT!

"Is everyone ready for action today?" Uncle Merle said when he joined the others at the kitchen table. "Sally, Mr. Wood asks us to meet with the planning committee after they finish the lionfish count. We can study the results and make some recommendations."

"Everyone seems eager to get started with some solutions," Aunt Sally said.

"Yes," Uncle Merle agreed. "I suspect that the divers are ready to just get out there and have a fish kill."

The group ate in silence for a few minutes. "I don't want to go see the divers kill the lionfish," Susan blurted. "I know they have to do something. There's a big problem. But I'm just not going out there to see it," she said, tears forming in her eyes.

"It's all right," Aunt Sally said, smiling at Susan. "I'm not planning to join the fish kill, either, although I understand how it will help solve the problem. We will study the information and make suggestions. That's our part."

"Susan," Uncle Merle said, casting a glance at Aunt Sally. "Why don't you and your Aunt Sally go out and get that count on the left side of the breakwater. Eric and I will help at the reef and meet you around noon to get your numbers. I am interested in the facts and the solutions we will come up with." He handed her a bag of yellow tape and stakes.

Uncle Merle and Eric gathered their gear and

headed to the car. "And she even helped me this morning with my picture captions," Susan heard Eric say when he jumped into the front seat and slammed the door. She smiled to herself.

Aunt Sally and Susan headed for the lagoon. They struggled into dive boots, fins, mask and snorkel. Aunt Sally handed Susan a pair of gloves. "I thought you might need to hold on to some rocks while we study the creatures. These can protect your hands. I noticed a minor cut on your index finger."

"It's nothing," Susan said. She took the gloves and slipped them over her hands. "These are really nice," she said. "Thank you."

"Let's go," Aunt Sally said. "Please take this slate so we can write our numbers down." Susan took it and put the pencil into the plastic tubing that formed a loop at the top of the slate.

"OK," Susan said, pushing off and kicking her fins. Aunt Sally slithered along beside her. She turned and smiled at Susan and gave her the OK sign that divers always use to let their partners know their equipment works well and they are ready to descend. They crossed the sunlit lagoon and moved up to the breakwater, staying far away from the channel.

Aunt Sally drove a short stake into the sand and tied one end of a plastic yellow tape to it. She handed the box with the coiled-up tape in it to Susan. As Susan swam along the face of the breakwater, she pulled the box, and the tape uncoiled. Every fifty feet Aunt Sally added a stake to keep it in place.

We're taking this count just the way divers do in the reef, Susan thought. *The scientists can use our information the help them decide on a plan to save the reef.* She paused while Aunt Sally reached out and wrote, "five hundred feet" on the slate Susan held. She signaled Susan to stand up.

"Let's count in segments, then add them up when we're done, just in case we want to stop or see something else that catches our attention," Aunt Sally laughed.

She knows me, Susan thought, nodding her head to show she agreed.

They turned and advanced slowly along, pulling the tape and searching the overhangs and cracks in the rock wall. They stopped frequently and Aunt Sally put up her fingers to show how many lionfish she saw. Susan showed her count on her fingers. They agreed with Aunt Sally's tally. *There are far too many,* she thought, moving along and hoping she wouldn't see any small fish disappear.

Thirty feet before they reached the channel, Aunt Sally stopped and signaled for Susan to stand up.

Susan smiled. Aunt Sally had used the hand sign for 'ascend' that divers use. She closed her fist and extended her thumb, jerking it up and down. *When you're in the water, you use hand signals to exchange information,* she thought to herself, smiling. She stood up and removed her mask and snorkel.

Aunt Sally took the slate and added up their numbers. "That's twenty fish," she said.

"Twenty fish living along five hundred feet of habitat," Susan said, frowning.

Aunt Sally studied the numbers. She looked at the row of rocks that harbored many small fish, corals and other creatures. "We could only cover the shoreward side of the breakwater," she said. "The next time we come out here there probably won't be any life," she mumbled.

"Let's head in," Aunt Sally said. "We can swim back along the breakwater and collect the tape and stakes, then head across the lagoon."

When they finally reached the shore in front of the hotel, they stood up and removed their snorkel gear. Aunt Sally said, "I have an idea. Come on."

"Gather your dive gear," Aunt Sally instructed as they entered the hotel. She excused herself and headed for the kitchen. Susan heard her talking on the phone. "We can be ready in an hour," Susan heard her say.

"Pastor McDonald has agreed to take us to the shallow reef just beyond Stingray City," she said. "I think it's time to look around and enjoy the sea for a while before the guys return."

Susan and Aunt Sally had just enough time to

grab a sandwich before Pastor McDonald arrived. It took less than an hour to reach Rum Point and head for the reef. Pastor McDonald stopped the boat and attached it to a buoy anchored deep in the sand just beyond the reef line. Soon Aunt Sally and Susan prepared to enter the sea by falling off the boat, backwards, into the water.

The cool sea surrounded Susan. She felt herself rise to the surface and saw Aunt Sally burst through. They gave each other the OK signal. Susan released air from her BCD vest and pinched her nose, blowing gently to clear both ears as she descended.

Aunt Sally gave the 'follow me' signal. Soon Aunt Sally stopped in front of a ledge and studied the area. Susan swam up beside her and stared. At first, she didn't see anything interesting, but a sudden movement in the shadow of the overhanging coral caught her attention. Something poked out and stared at her. The creature had a triangular body no bigger than the end of her finger. It looked like the Creator had taken ahold of one end of the triangle and pulled it until it became a long point. Two miniature bubble eyes sat on each side of the point, halfway up. *They are so small. How can they really see?* Susan thought. *But they see me.*

Susan imagined how God attached eight spider-like legs to the crab's body. They looked at least three times as long as the body was wide. Each leg bends with a tiny joint. *It's genius,* she thought. Susan glanced over at Aunt Sally. She smiled and her eyes glowed. Susan swallowed a laugh. Water sloshed around in Aunt Sally's mask. *She always gets water in her mask when she smiles,* Susan thought. *She says it gets in through her smile wrinkles.*

Aunt Sally pressed the heel of her hand against the top of her mask and blew out into it. The water escaped, leaving her mask dry.

Aunt Sally pointed to Susan's slate. Susan handed it to her. "Arrow Crab," she wrote.

Susan smiled. She drew a picture of the creature. She sketched the triangular body, the bubble eyes and the spindly legs. That's when she noticed two shorter appendages that acted like arms with real elbows. Two purple claws sat at the end of each one. They picked at the coral and the sea floor, jamming something into the slit mouth. She couldn't contain herself, threw back her head and laughed. Water trickled into her mask. She didn't care. She knew how to clear it when she wanted to.

"Adorable!" she wrote on her slate when she could see clearly again. Aunt Sally nodded in agreement. At that moment, as if awakened by the noise outside its home, another creature appeared. Susan stared. It looked somewhat larger than the Arrow Crab. It had the shape of a shrimp, yet very tiny.

Aunt Sally took the slate again. "Banded Coral

Shrimp," she wrote. "It cleans. Watch!"

Susan stared at the miniature red-and-white-banded creature. She counted two pairs of very long, white, hair-like antennae that twitched about. The shrimp waved a pair of tiny, long legs that ended in white claws. It seemed to dance about in the entrance of a cave covered by a flat coral formation.

Aunt Sally tapped Susan's hand. She removed Susan's glove and pointed to the cut on one finger. Then she pushed her hand toward the shrimp.

Susan held still, wondering what would happen. The shrimp didn't look big enough to hurt her. It touched her hand with two long antennae that tickled her skin. Soon it inched out from the ledge and crawled over her hand. Susan felt like screaming and throwing the shrimp off, but held her arm still.

The shrimp stopped when it reached the minor cut on her finger. It did something to the cut. It felt like a tiny sting. *This creature is cleaning my cut,* she thought. Susan almost forgot to breathe as the shrimp moved over her hand, checking each cuticle. Then it scampered away under the ledge. Susan could only see the long, white antennae sticking out.

At this moment, an overwhelming emotion flooded through Susan's mind. *What kind of wonderful Creator do I have that could make such creatures and hide them in the bottom of the sea?* she thought. They protect the reef by keeping the fish and other creatures clean. Love filled her heart and tears formed in her eyes and threatened to spill over. She looked up at Aunt Sally, who smiled at her. They just hung there in the water, looking at the tiny legs of the crabs sticking out from under the ledge.

Aunt Sally checked her dive computer and signaled to Susan to begin her ascent. Susan gave her the OK signal and pushed the button that slowly pumped air into her BCD vest. She pointed her hand up and rose very slowly with Aunt Sally, to the surface. Neither of them spoke during the trip back to the boat dock and to their hotel. So many thoughts swirled around in Susan's head. She kept reliving the feeling of the wisp of a creature prancing about on her hand, and thinking of the Creator who designed it.

"Thank you for taking us to the reef," Aunt Sally said to Pastor McDonald. "I think my plan to help Susan is coming along. She looked pretty amazed at the shrimp and the crab I showed her today."

"Good," Pastor McDonald said. "Let me know how I can help you with your plan."

Susan showered and changed into dry clothes. She could hear Aunt Sally singing. *It's so amazing.* Susan thought. *I feel so full of joy and that I love the whole world.*

Susan took the stairs two at a time. She plunked herself onto the living room couch. She could hardly wait for Aunt Sally to finish her shower. After what seemed like forever, she heard her come down the stairs. She joined Susan in the living room.

"That was quite a dive," she said, curling up next to Susan on the couch.

"I know," Susan said, jumping up and whirling around the room, then dropping onto the couch next to Aunt Sally without saying another word.

"Susan," Aunt Sally said, "You are just experiencing what I have learned to call The, 'affection factor.' This is the second thing that happens when we go out into God's creation. The first factor tells us how nature captures your attention." She picked up the paper she had written on the day during worship and scribbled something. She held it up for Susan to see.

1. Nature grabs your attention and captures your curiosity.

2. Nature lifts your affections up to God, the Creator.

"God actually designed for this to happen," she said. "This 'affection factor' kicks in as you begin to enjoy God's creation. Your heart opens up to Him. You are now ready to..."

"I saw the most unbelievable thing out there," Eric shouted as he burst through the door and dropped a pile of wet gear onto the floor. He saw Susan in the living room and plunked down beside her. "There's a crab that looks like some outer space creature with bubble eyes so small I can hardly believe it can actually see stuff. It can, though, because it stared right at me and touched me with legs so long and skinny it makes all spiders look fat."

"I saw…" Susan began.

"It pranced around on tiptoe. That's when I saw that the creature had two shorter legs that ended in…"

"Purple claws," Susan said. "I saw it too. And, it often lives near the other crazy, cute crab called the Banded Coral Shrimp."

"That's the one that cleans all kinds of creatures that come to it for detailing," Eric laughed. "Uncle Merle said that these little guys are so important to the reef that if removed, the fish will go to other areas of the reef to live. Who but a God like ours would think of such things? I'm really amazed."

"The miracle of the 'affection factor' has him," Aunt Sally laughed. "I think we need to talk more about this," Aunt Sally said, motioning for Uncle Merle to sit down.

"What factor?" Eric said, smoothing a shock of blond hair from his face.

"The 'affection factor' is the second thing that happens to those who go out and enjoy God's creations," Uncle Merle said. "Do you remember the first thing?" He said yawning.

"How can I forget?" Eric said. "Nature grabs the

125

attention. Susan was mumbling it when she fell asleep last night."

"Something else happens after that," Aunt Sally said. "Can you guess what it is?"

"Well," Eric hesitated, looking down at his hands. "I feel pretty happy right now."

"Do you feel like you love the whole world?" Susan asked.

"Maybe not the whole world," Eric said. "But I have been thinking about what a fantastic Creator we have. When I saw that Arrow Crab with those two bubble eyes, I laughed so hard my mask leaked."

"Aunt Sally," Susan said, becoming serious. "What is so important about This factor? What's it meant to do?"

"When God has your attention, and your heart is full of affection for Him, what do you think you are ready to do?" Aunt Sally questioned.

Susan and Eric sat quietly for long moments. "Learn," Eric said, jumping to his feet. "I'm ready to learn."

"He is right," Uncle Merle said, reaching out and wrapping his arms around Aunt Sally. "Watching these kids discover this stuff is so great."

"I'm ready to learn about everything that God has made," Eric said. He turned and gazed out at the sea. "And I want to capture it all on film."

"I want to write about it," Susan said, standing up

and moving beside Eric. "I don't want my gift to be used on anything else."

They watched the sun hesitate on the horizon, sizzling red, and disappear. "Nothing else I've ever experienced is this good," Eric said. "I've discovered how God uses nature to teach me wonderful things."

"Once God has your attention, and your heart is open to Him, you are ready to learn. So, you could say that nature teaches us truth." She picked up the sheet of paper and added to the list.

1. Nature grabs your attention and captures your curiosity.

2. Nature lifts your affections to God.

3. Nature teaches you truth. The mind is ready to learn.

"They can't wait for number four," Uncle Merle said.

"Would you mind if we had a sleep break between our adventures?" Aunt Sally asked.

"Let's meet at 8:00 for breakfast and take some time to talk before we go diving," Uncle Merle said, following the twins up the stairs.

"It's miraculous," Eric said, pausing at Susan's door.

"I know," she agreed. She entered her room and fell across the bed.

Eric smiled. He went into his room, put his pajamas on and climbed into bed. He wanted to see the images of crabs again in his imagination, but next thing he knew Susan was pounding on his door.

"Get up, Eric. Aunt Sally is calling us to breakfast," she said. "I want to find out what the fourth thing that nature does."

Eric opened his eyes. A broad smile spread across his face. *This is going to be one perfect day*, he thought. There are so many new things to discover.

CHAPTER 10

STRATEGY

"How about a report concerning the lionfish count completed yesterday?" Aunt Sally asked as the family gathered around the table the next morning for breakfast. "I've made your favorite fruit toast, Eric."

"It smells good," Eric said, dropping two pieces of toast onto his plate and scooping a heaping spoonful of sauce. He loved the raspberries and blueberries that Aunt Sally always put in the sauce. He added a squeeze of honey. "Perfect!" he said. "Thanks, Aunt Sally."

"The count is complete," Aunt Sally said. "All the counters have turned in their data. These lionfish are just everywhere. They especially congregate in the shallow reefs."

"It is so troubling," Uncle Merle said. "No one can come up with a perfect solution."

"Several scientists have made suggestions, but none of these come close to curing the problem." Aunt Sally said. "The lionfish have intruded into every reef system. There are no predators to keep them in check. They reproduce frequently. They have voracious appetites, eating almost anything they can suck into their mouths. It seems impossible to eradicate them. The committee looked at the count, explored potential solutions and made their recommendation."

"What will they do?" Eric asked.

"Teams of divers will go out and kill as many as they can. This will keep the lionfish in check," Uncle Merle said. "They will use special three-pronged harpoons to capture the fish, then stuff them into large plastic tubes. They will bring them to collection centers," Uncle Merle explained. "We hope that this will lessen the number of the lionfish in the reef system and give the young fish a chance to mature."

"Don't get discouraged," Aunt Sally said, looking at Susan's and Eric's gloomy faces. "No one is giving up on this. They hope to discover a better solution."

They sat in silence for a few minutes. *I hope they discover an answer soon,* Susan thought. A sad feeling flooded over her when she thought of the young fish being sucked into the lionfish's mouths.

"Speaking of discovery," Eric said, breaking the silence. "I know that God uses nature to catch our attention and lift our affections to Him. Then, He uses it to teach us something important. This discovery is really important to me, but, I just can't figure out the last part of His plan."

"I want to know what number four is, too," Susan said, brightening up. "I could use some good news right now."

"Before we explain number four," Aunt Sally said, "I want to draw your attention to something important. Each creature has a special lesson hidden within its life cycle or habits. Sometimes this is obvious, but at other times it takes genuine effort to determine it. I believe that we can pray and expect that God will help us understand and discover His lessons. This is always a splendid adventure."

"The Word of God teaches the same thing that nature does. I like to think that the Word is the written Bible, and that nature is the visual Bible." Uncle Merle said. "It helps us see and touch things that make the Bible clear to us."

"I see that now," Susan said. "I wrote about the Venus Tower and discovered that the Bible teaches us that Jesus is our Tower in Proverbs 18:10. 'The Lord is like a strong Tower. The righteous run to it and are saved.'"

Eric's face lit up. "You remembered the Tower, and the location of the verse?"

"I remember the whole story," Susan said. "I even remember the lesson."

"This is exciting, Susan. While number three is about learning, number four is about..." Aunt Sally began, giving Eric, who sat on the edge of his chair, a chance to finish her sentence.

"Remembering!" he almost shouted. "That's how God's strategy finishes. He helps us remember. And Susan did just that. She could even tell us where to find the verse. Hey, does this work with stuff like history?"

"It does," Uncle Merle said, laughing. "It does because when an idea attaches to an adventure with some kind of visual, you always remember. We call it, anchoring."

"How does that work?" Susan asked.

"When the lesson or idea anchors to an object, something wonderful happens." Uncle Merle said. "When you see the object, you remember everything. It just happened right now."

Aunt Sally reached over to the counter and picked up her computer. She opened a file called Nature Lessons. "That's the Venus Tower," Susan said, pulling her chair closer to the computer. Her eyes got wide with a new idea.

"She's remembering all the details of where it

lives in the bottom of the sea and how it's tied down with byssus threads," Aunt Sally said. "Am I right? Susan?"

"Yes," Susan said, leaning close to the screen. "But something else also happens," she said, looking at Aunt Sally.

"What is it?" Aunt Sally questioned.

"I remember just how I felt when you told us the beautiful story. I feel the boat sloshing on the water, I see the sparkling water and I imagine the darkness that the little creature had to live in. I felt frightened that it was so small and the sea so big."

"Anything else?" Uncle Merle encouraged.

"I felt so glad to know God provided a safe home for the tiny creature."

"Are you saying that you really felt all those things again, right now?" Eric said.

"Just seeing the picture made me remember how I felt," Susan said. "Wow!"

Aunt Sally sat silently. A smile spread across her face. She reached out and took Susan's hand. "I know you did. This is the strategy God uses to imprint truth about Him in both your mind or intelligence and..."

"In my heart," Susan finished, sighing. "It's in my heart, too."

"So, number four is this," Aunt Sally said. "Nature anchors truth in the mind and the heart or emotions."

"Add it to the list," Susan said, getting up and heading to the living room.

Aunt Sally picked the computer up and took it with her into the living room. She set it on the lamp table. Everyone gathered around her. She wrote, '4 Nature anchors truth in the mind and heart', on the sheet of paper Susan handed her.

"Let's experiment and see just how this works," she said, clicking on another file. Up popped a picture of Susan, Eric, and Uncle Merle leaping off a cliff into the sea.

"Our awful trip down current when the dive lights blinked off and left us in darkness," Susan shouted. "I felt scared."

"The new lights changed everything. We learned that a small light means lots of fear, but a big light means much less fear," Eric added.

"I remember, Merle," Aunt Sally said, smiling. "You told me you almost jumped out of your skin when the twins grabbed you." Everyone agreed.

Aunt Sally clicked another file button. A beautiful Queen Conch appeared on the screen. The picture showed Susan about to pick it up from the sand. Eric laughed. He reached over and yanked Susan's ponytail.

"The shock on your face, when the Mexican man brought that hammer down on your treasure, was a sight," Eric said. Everyone laughed except Susan.

"You're supposed to remember the lesson," Susan said, putting her hands on her hips and glaring at Eric. She could hardly keep herself from bursting into laughter.

"I remember it all right," Eric said. "When you don't communicate, stuff gets broken."

"We could give that more thought and see what God's Word says about communication, especially with Him, the expert," Aunt Sally suggested.

"I was thinking of that verse in second Timothy, chapter one, verse 12. Paul says, with some emphasis, 'I know in whom I have believed and know that He is able to keep everything I've entrusted to Him until the day I see Him face to face,'" Uncle Merle said.

"You must admit that you gave your treasure into the hands of someone you didn't know and who didn't know what you wanted," Aunt Sally said.

"She sure did," Eric teased. "I bet you could give us a rundown on how you felt when you saw the shell shattered to pieces."

Susan looked down at her feet. She remembered. She sighed. Everyone looked at her, but no one spoke for a moment.

"It gives us a good example of the anchoring of truth," Uncle Merle said, clearing his throat. "You remembered even your sad feelings."

"Let's look at another example," Aunt Sally

suggested, turning their attention to the screen. She clicked on a file marked, "Southern Stingray."

The twins shouted out the sights they remembered and the feelings they experienced, as fast as they could. "That was easy because it was so recent," Aunt Sally said, "The good news is that even the passing of time won't cause you to forget. Even if you want to forget, you won't."

"Remember, tomorrow is Sabbath, our last day here," Uncle Merle said after they sat quietly for a moment. "We won't dive anywhere because we must wait twenty-four hours before we fly. But I thought you would like to visit the Turtle Farm. I've taken care of all the fees ahead of time and let the director know about our visit. You can hold a turtle and ask questions."

"Have you told the twins about our strategy for today?" Aunt Sally asked.

"One of the volunteer divers, named Jim, told me about a Caribbean Reef Octopus that he sees every time he visits in a certain part of the reef in the early evening and again at night. He thinks we have a good chance of seeing it if we go out at sunset. Eric, take the movie camera and get all the footage you can. Susan, you could write about the encounter. We could call it, Our Strategy Adventure." Uncle Merle said.

"Your aim will be to discover the escape strategy

exhibited by the octopus when we disturb it. Take your dive slate so you can take a few notes, Susan," Aunt Sally instructed.

"I'd rather not dive right now," Susan said, staring at her feet.

"It should be a beautiful way to bring in the Sabbath," Aunt Sally said, "We will study nature and have the reef and the boat to ourselves."

"I know," Susan said. "I just don't feel like meeting up with the divers killing fish."

"Divers have already cleared this section of the reef of every lionfish they could find." Uncle Merle explained.

"I don't think we will see a single diver trying to catch a fish," Aunt Sally added. "And, I think you will enjoy this dive because we can begin before the sun sets so you can record the octopus and its strategy."

"Okay," Susan said, bounding up the stairs to gather her dive gear. *I better take an extra light,* she thought.

Uncle Merle led them to a boat tied up at the far end of the dock in front of the hotel. "Hello," a tall man wearing a white hat, said. "I'm Captain George. Welcome aboard the *Island Explorer*." He helped them carry their gear onto the boat and hook up four tanks to their BCD vests. He checked each piece of equipment carefully.

INTRUDER ALERT!

In less than twenty minutes, they reached a section of Babylon reef near the buoy Jim had described.

"Gear up!" Uncle Merle said, struggling into his dive skins.

Soon they perched on the dive platform and Aunt Sally called, "leap." Each one put their right foot out and leaped into the sea, clicking on their dive lights. All four surfaced, gave the OK dive signal. They sank down just as the sun disappeared below the horizon.

Twenty-five feet below, they leveled off beside a beautiful reef where the sea fans waved in the gentle current and schools of fish swirled past.

Uncle Merle gave them the sign for 'follow me' and they swam in a line, staring at the reef in the dimming light. Five minutes later, Uncle Merle signaled for them to stop. He pointed to a crevice in the reef and shone his UK 400 light into the space between two brain corals. Two green and brown tentacles stretched themselves out, followed by two more. An oblong head the size of Eric's fist popped out. Two bubble eyes sat perched on top of the head and two more tentacles appeared. They curled up and stretched out, poking into a nearby crevice, each acting independent of the other.

"The octopus crammed into tight space to hide" Susan wrote on her slate. Eric followed the octopus as it oozed along. Uncle Merle pushed ahead, shining his light at the creature that changed from brown to greenish-red. It almost disappeared from sight and became the color of the surrounding reef.

"It changed color and almost disappeared," Susan scribbled. She smiled when Uncle Merle moved in close with his light.

Maybe it has found a deep enough hiding place and it won't come out again, Susan thought. Suddenly the little octopus darted into the open, tentacle seven and eight joining the six already swirling about, each in different directions. It shot a stream of black ink that hid it from them in the dimming light. Then it streaked out into the dark water and all tentacles turning backwards in a jet-like fashion. The octopus paused a moment and dove for a deep crevice between two coral heads. No amount of light would force it out into the open again.

"The octopus shot ink around itself. It hid from us a moment, then took off." Susan wrote.

They huddled around the crevice where the octopus hid and waited. "This is foraging time," Uncle Merle wrote on his slate. "It might come out again if we back off."

They waited as the water darkened, but the octopus stayed put. Soon Uncle Merle gave the thumbs up signal for them to ascend. They rose together and plunged through the surface. The boat sat on a glassy sea a few feet away. A full moon shone down on them, as bright as an extra dive light.

"It's so lovely on a night like this," Aunt Sally said, removing her mask and just hanging in the water.

"I got four strategies," Susan said. "And it looks like Eric took a lot of great clips."

"Read me your list," Uncle Merle said, moving toward the dive ladder.

"The first thing the octopus did," Susan explained, "is that it hid. How it ever squeezed into such small places is a mystery to me."

"The octopus doesn't have a bunch of bones inside. That's why it can push itself into tiny hiding places," Eric said, climbing the dive ladder and removing his tank and other gear.

"Then the octopus checked out a new hiding place so it could escape that awful light," Susan added. She handed Captain George her fins and climbed aboard.

"I love the way every tentacle acts on its own," Aunt Sally said. "I wonder if that means that it could actually do eight things at once?" she said, gasping.

"Next it tried to jet away into the distance. Of course, that didn't work either," Susan said, sitting down on one of the boat seats and dropping her mask into her gear bag.

Captain George passed around a glass of fruit juice for each of them as soon as they all had settled in the boat and dropped wet gear into their dive bags. "Enjoy", he said, "We aren't in any hurry."

"Let's sing a bit," Aunt Sally suggested, "then finish our discussion."

They chose all the songs they could remember that included the sea or nature and watched the moon move higher in the sky. It seemed to smile down on them. "What do you think of the Creator's strategy for keeping an octopus safe?" Uncle Merle finally said.

"That octopus is a real escape artist. I'll learn more when I watch the clips I took," Eric admitted. "That little guy kept me pretty busy."

"We have seen a lot this week," Aunt Sally said. "We met an intruder that causes problems everywhere in the reef."

"Aunt Sally," Susan said, gazing up at the stream of moonlight that painted a path across the sea. "I enjoyed learning about God's strategy to help us know Him. I can see how important it is to study God's Word and learn to read the book of nature." She paused a moment and a big smile lit her face up. "So, was it your strategy to teach me how to manage my intruder?"

"Or keep intruders out in the first place," Eric said. Everyone nodded in agreement.

"Susan, I thought you would trade in your paperback intruder for a better plan," Aunt Sally said. "You can see that Satan has a strategy of his own. He tries to determine what we want and need that is totally good and right. Then he offers us something that fills our need, but will hurt us or separate us from God."

"It looks like two different powers are interested in snagging our attention," Uncle Merle said. "I think Susan shows courage in the way she handles her intruder."

"She shut off Satan's influence and then opened her mind and heart to God who loves her and wants to give her a productive and joyful life. This will help her reach out and touch other's lives with power."

"Is all the gear stowed?" Captain George asked. "I'll release the anchor from the buoy, rev this motor up and head for the dock. I'll see you all at church tomorrow."

"This has been a perfect day," Eric said. "Thank you for bringing us here," he said to Uncle Merle and Aunt Sally. "I know you had a strategy in mind. It sure worked." He joined Susan at the back of the boat where she sat, letting the warm wind blow through her hair.

"I'm glad you figured out stuff about the intruder," He shouted into the wind.

"Thanks!" Susan screamed back. She knew Eric heard her in spite of the wind blowing around them, because he smiled.

STRATEGY

"I want to find a better way to be an excellent writer!" she shouted.

"You will," Eric said. "Aunt Sally has a strategy."

"Aunt Sally has a strategy," she repeated the words to herself, smiling. She tried to imagine what else Aunt Sally's strategy included, but her thoughts blew away on the wind as The *Island Explorer* tossed up sea spray and followed the moon's path toward shore.

CHAPTER 11

THE PERFECT PLAN

"Hurry, Eric. Let's go," Susan said, grabbing the back of Eric's shirt and pulling him toward the car.

Aunt Sally and Uncle Merle took another ten minutes to talk with friends before they left the church. They headed for the parking lot and climbed into the car with the twins.

"Green Turtles are the biggest turtles in the ocean," Susan said, leaning over the front seat. "Except for the Leatherback Turtle. He weighs up to 2,000 pounds. I'm glad we got to see some of the friends we made on our last visit to Cayman, Aunt Sally, but I can't wait to see those green turtles."

"The turtles aren't green, Susan," Eric corrected. "They have some greenish fat on their bodies, but they aren't green. But I'm going to turn green if I don't get some food soon."

"I'm sure they'll look just like the ones we saw in the reef," Susan said. "We can get a closer look at them at the farm."

"These turtles will be a lot larger than any you saw in the reef," Uncle Merle said, as they pulled up to the hotel.

Everyone ate lunch quickly and headed for the turtle farm.

"They don't call it a farm now," Aunt Sally said. "Look. The sign says, 'Cayman Turtle Centre, Island Wildlife Encounter.'"

"Isn't the word Centre spelled wrong?" Susan asked.

"That's the Old French way of saying it," Aunt Sally said.

"Let's go to the turtle tanks first," Eric said, adjusting his camera and heading for an assortment of round tanks that sat nearby.

Susan and Eric stopped at one of the large, open-air water tanks and peered in.

"Look at these little turtles," Susan shouted as Aunt Sally and Uncle Merle came up beside them. "I see at least twenty of them. The colors of their shells shine so brightly."

"The water in these tanks looks very clean," Aunt Sally said, swishing her hands in the salt water as the turtles passed by.

"Notice that each tank holds turtles of about the same size and age," Uncle Merle explained. He reached into the tank and picked up a dinner-plate size turtle. It flapped its front flippers, hitting Uncle Merle's arms. Aunt Sally reached over and stroked the turtle's throat and it calmed down.

"Wow!" Eric said, taking a movie clip of the action. "Susan, you pick one up and try that," he instructed.

Susan reached into the tank and picked up a turtle, placing one hand on each side of the shell. She held it up for Eric to see. The front flippers waved about, smacking her arms. "Ouch! That really hurts," she said.

Aunt Sally reached over and stroked the turtle under its chin. The turtle calmed down. "It also works if you turn the turtle over."

"Thanks," Susan said, smiling. "This turtle is beautiful. It's hard to believe that this little creature can live for over eighty years."

"I guess being around all that water gives it a long life," Eric said, laughing.

They walked around the tanks, picking up turtles of different sizes. Suddenly, they faced a beautiful, natural lagoon. A cluster of large turtles swam slowly by.

"Look at that," Eric shouted. "These guys are giants."

Susan looked over the railing into the lagoon. "Uncle Merle, you're right. I didn't see any turtles in the reef half this size."

"These turtles are mature adults," Uncle Merle explained. "They probably each weigh over three hundred pounds."

"Scientists consider Green Turtles endangered," Aunt Sally said. "Naturalists observe them on the coasts of over one hundred and forty countries, so humans haven't destroyed them all. I think the Turtle Centre raises hundreds of turtles and puts them back into the sea. They can control whether the turtles will be male or female with temperature. Some eggs are placed in incubators with the temperature set above eighty degrees. These hatch out female turtles. To hatch male turtles, they just lower the thermostat."

"After the females dig holes with their back flippers and deposit the eggs, they cover them up with sand. The workers here at the Centre dig the eggs up and put them into an incubator," Uncle Merle explained.

"Look," Susan said. "The turtles have their own beach. Some of these females will lay eggs right here on this beach, so they won't have a long trip to find the place where they were born."

"That's true," Uncle Merle laughed. "God gave them an amazing ability to travel thousands of miles through the sea to find the same beach where they hatched. No one really understands how this happens."

Susan and Eric spotted a wading pool and ran off to check it out. Small turtles swam about in the clear water. Aunt Sally and Uncle Merle followed them.

"Take off your shoes and go into the pool. You can walk around with the turtles. They won't hurt you," the twins heard a man say to his young daughter. She sat down and removed her shoes and socks.

"Go ahead," the man said. "I'll take your picture."

Susan and Eric moved close to the man. They watched the girl wade into the shallow water. She wore yellow shorts and a shirt with a picture of a turtle on the front. Someone had tied up her ponytail with a yellow ribbon.

"Is she afraid?" Susan asked. "The turtles are swimming all around her."

"No. Abby is only six, but she just loves turtles," the man explained. "By the way, I'm Mr. Barns and this is my daughter, Abby."

"My name is Susan, and that's my twin brother, Eric," Susan said. "This is my Uncle Merle and my Aunt Sally." The adults shook hands. They watched Abby among with the turtles. She giggled and splashed in the water. She followed one turtle after another. They didn't swim away when she reached out and touched them. "Jesus made them so beautiful," she said, looking up at her father.

"Just like you," he called out. "When this little turtle grows up, it will swim all over the ocean and find its way right back here to have its own babies," he explained.

Suddenly the girl stood still, tears trickled down her face.

Eric stared at Abby. He thrust his camera into Susan's hands and took off his shoes and socks. He waded into the pool and stood beside the girl.

"I'm Eric," he said. "Don't be afraid."

Susan pushed the button on the camera and focused on the girl and Eric. *He'll wish I had taken pictures,* she thought.

"I'm Abby," The girl said, sniffing. "I'm not afraid of the turtles. I just wish my mommy was here to see them."

"I'm sorry she isn't here," Eric said. "Where is she?" he asked.

"She died," Abby said. "She can't come here."

"Oh," Eric said. "You must miss her a lot."

Abby stared at her feet and a fresh supply of tears rolled down her cheeks.

"Are you afraid the turtles will get lost out there in the middle of the ocean?" Eric asked.

"They don't have anyone to show them the way. They don't have a mother," Abby said.

"No, they don't," Eric said, casting a glance up at Susan. "But they have instinct," Eric said, brightening. "It's something in their brain that tells them how to get where they want to go. That's why they aren't afraid."

"I'm afraid," Abby said.

"I feel afraid sometimes," Eric admitted. "My mother died, too. She couldn't come here with us. I miss her. Susan and I didn't know what to do when Mother died. We didn't know where home was. But God guided us. Aunt Sally and Uncle Merle made us part of their family."

"Did He talk to you?" Abby asked.

"I didn't hear Him speaking," Eric said. "But He spoke to our hearts and minds, just like He does to the little turtle. It's a miracle."

Mr. Barns smiled and looked at Aunt Sally and Uncle Merle. "A fine boy you have there," he said.

"It's amazing how kids can help each other," Uncle Merle said, placing his hand on Mr. Barn's shoulder.

"It's happening," Susan said to Aunt Sally, dancing about.

"It is," Aunt Sally agreed. "It really is."

"The four secrets are working right before our eyes. Look how those turtles have captured Abby's attention."

"I think that 'affection factor' has kicked in, too," Aunt Sally said, smiling.

"She will soon discover the truth. God guides the turtle, and He wants to guide her, too," Susan said.

"I bet this will be an unforgettable experience," Aunt Sally said.

"She's going to remember it every time she sees a turtle." Susan said. "That's the miracle of anchoring."

"Excuse me," the man said, moving up beside Susan. "I heard you talking about four secrets. You look excited. What is that all about?"

"Eric and I learned about the four secret powers that nature has to help us know God better. The first one is that it captures the attention," Susan said. "The turtles have her attention."

"True," Mr. Barns said. "I have tried other things to help her work through her grief. Nature always works the best. It opens her heart right up."

"That's because the 'affection factor' has kicked in," Susan laughed.

"The 'affection factor'?" Mr. Barns asked.

"See how she loves the turtles. God is using them to open her heart to His love."

"Then what happens?" Mr. Barns asked.

"When a person's heart is open, nature can teach truth," Susan continued. "The turtle can show her that God is like a guide. He knows the best way for her to travel through her life, even though she doesn't have a mother. Of course," Susan said, "It sure helps to have a father who loves her."

"So, you're saying that I can teach my daughter

about guidance by helping her see how God works with His sea turtles," the man said.

"Yes," Susan said.

"Listen," Mr. Barns said, "I am interested in learning more about your concepts about nature. I'm the editor of a Christian youth magazine that focuses on helping young people learn from nature. I'm here with my daughter, so I am busy right now, but would you call me when you get stateside?" Mr. Barns reached out and handed Uncle Merle a business card.

"We are heading home in the morning," Uncle Merle said. "We will get in touch with you."

"Daddy," Abby called, splashing out of the wading pool. "I'm a miracle. I won't get lost even if I feel like I'm all by myself sometimes. The turtle has instinct, so it won't get lost, either."

"You are a miracle," Mr. Barns said, reaching out and scooping Abby up into his arms. She dripped water all over him, but he didn't complain. "You are my little miracle."

"Don't you have even a little instinct?" he teased.

"Of course not," Abby said, placing her small hands on each of her father's cheeks. "I'm not a turtle. I'm a girl. I have Jesus." Everyone laughed and nodded their heads in agreement.

"Eric," Mr. Barns said, wiping water from his face. He turned to Eric as he climbed out of the wading pool and pulled his socks and shoes on. "I couldn't help but noticed your nice camera equipment. I'll bet you're are a whiz with photograpy. Would you be willing to send pictures with a story I'm going ask Susan to write?"

"Yes, Sir," Eric said. "We always work together."

"I must leave you all now, but please make contact when with me when you get home. I will wait to hear from you. Eric, thanks for talking with Abby," he said, placing his hand on Eric's shoulder.

"You're welcome, Sir," Eric said, looking down at his feet.

"Goodbye then," Mr. Barns called as they walked toward the entrance to the Turtle Centre.

"Goodbye, Eric," Abby called.

"We saw it happen," Susan said, jumping about. "We saw it, didn't we, Aunt Sally?"

"We did," Aunt Sally agreed. "Eric, you let God use you to make it happen. Without really planning it, you helped Abby experience the four secrets. I am proud of you," she smiled.

"This is God's perfect plan," Susan said as they climbed into the car and headed for the hotel four hours later.

"What do you mean?" Aunt Sally questioned.

"First, we learn, then we teach others. Nature is the wonderful helper," Susan said. "That's part of God's plan." *It's a perfect plan,* Susan thought to

153

herself. *And he wants me to be part of it.*

"Do you think that man was serious about our writing an article and illustrating it with Eric's pictures?" Susan asked later when they entered the hotel.

"I do," Aunt Sally said. "God has a way of opening doors to encourage us to move in a direction He has chosen. Supper in thirty minutes," she added.

Thirty minutes later they gathered in the kitchen. Aunt Sally prepared her famous haystacks. Susan and Eric piled corn chips onto their plates and smothered them with Mexican beans. They added tomatoes, onions, avocado, and Aunt Sally's special spicy sauce. No one spoke for several minutes. Suddenly they heard a ping sound from the computer in the living room.

"I guess we have a message," Aunt Sally said. She got up from the table and walked into the living room. In a few minutes they heard the printer go off and Aunt Sally returned to the table. A smile spread itself over her face and her eyes danced.

"Good news?" Uncle Merle asked.

"It certainly is," Aunt Sally said. "God has His ways of moving a person forward. I see that He is doing that right now." She laughed.

"Read the message," Susan almost demanded. "I'm about to jump out of my skin."

"Try not to do that," Aunt Sally teased. "You

will make it impossible to do what this message is suggesting."

"Your class really enjoyed the story about the Venus Tower. They asked the teacher to read it twice. They want to know if you have any other object lessons like that one?"

"Wow!" Susan said.

"The most interesting thing is that the story not only caught their attention, but Miss Specks said it moved upon their hearts. During the discussion, several kids admitted that the story helped them think more about what kind of God we really have."

Susan stared at Aunt Sally. She got up from the table and looked out the living room window at the sea sparkling beneath the tropical sun. *Something I write can actually help people know God better,* she thought. *There isn't anything like it. I have never realized how I can make a difference.*

"We can make a difference or we can just entertain people," Susan blurted out, dashing up the stairs to her room.

"I imagine she has some thinking to do," Aunt Sally said.

"I'll help with the dishes," Eric said, picking up the plates from the table. "I figured out the same thing today in the wading pool," Eric admitted. "It felt good helping Abby. Nothing has ever felt that good before."

"Eric, why don't you go on upstairs, too. Uncle Merle and I left something special for you in your room. We will take over here in the kitchen." She smiled and watched Eric take the stairs two at a time.

Moments later, she heard him say, "Susan, Aunt Sally and Uncle Merle gave me a new program for editing pictures! It's a beauty. Look at all the options it gives me."

Susan stood in the doorway and looked at his computer screen. "It looks like you will have more tools and they will be easier to use," she said.

"Look on your pillow, Susan," Aunt Sally called up the stairs. She stood smiling beside Uncle Merle.

Susan disappeared into her room. She came out a moment later holding up a package of DVDs.

"What is it?" Eric said, leaping up from his chair. 'Creative Techniques for Christian Writers,' he read from the package. "It's an electronic class for beginning writers," he said.

The twins tumbled down the stairs into the arms of Aunt Sally and Uncle Merle.

"Thank-you," they chorused.

"We wanted you both to have tools to help you prepare for the work God is planning for you." Uncle Merle explained.

"Susan, this set of DVDs will help you discover good writing techniques from authors who love God and use their talents to help others know Him. You want to do more than entertain. You want to make a difference. I believe this is God's plan for you."

"With God's help, I will not allow anything or anyone intrude into God's plan for me," Susan said, wrapping her arms around Aunt Sally.

"This is a perfect time to talk with our Father in heaven," Uncle Merle said, drawing the group together.

"Father, we love you," Uncle Merle said. "Thank you for giving us each special talent. Help us use these gifts to teach others about how good you are. Protect us from Satan who always wants to intrude, steal our time and get us off course. Thank you for our family. Help all the other young people who are searching to realize that they have special God-given talents, too. Guide them. Help them know you can do anything and that you love them. We pray this in the name of Jesus. Amen."

"Amen," everyone chorused.

"There won't be any lionfish intruding into the reef of her life," Eric said, smiling at Susan.

"I don't think so," Aunt Sally said.

"I don't think so, either," Uncle Merle agreed

That's because I'm part of a plan, Susan thought to herself, *I'm part of a perfect plan.*

Treasures by the Sea
Book 1

Get set for adventure as Eric and Susan discover exciting truths about God's love. Discover that sea shells, sea stars, and fish do more than slither, crawl, and swish. They teach you about a God that loves you.

When a terrible accident takes the life of their mother, Eric and Susan are sent to California to live with Aunt Sally in her house by the sea.

They have lots of questions. Will we fit in here in California? Why did Mother have to die? Does God really care about us?

Together, they spend many hours with Aunt Sally, in and around the ocean. Soon, Eric and Susan begin to make new friends and discover answers to their questions.

Treasures by the Sea is the first in a series of Christian stories that help children understand the core beliefs of the Seventh-day Adventist Church and the Bible. Using her real life adventures in and around the Pacific Ocean, the author weaves lessons from nature and the Bible to help children understand God's messages of love for them.

Summer of the Sharks
Book 2

"Eleuthera." Eric said the name to himself. 'Freedom.' He wondered if the name really fit the island. He wished he could feel free - free from his fears.

When twelve-year-old twins Eric and Susan move in with their aunt, they never dream they will end up on a remote island paradise for a coral reef restoreation project. Susan bubbles over with excitement at the promise of underwater adventures. But the thought of cruising around in a large ocean full of creepy and dangerous creatures scares Eric. He tries to keep his fear a secret and makes excuses for staying behind.

The twins are soon swimming, snorkeling, and SNUBA diving in a dazzling undersea world. The living kaleidoscope teaches them scientific and spiritual lessons about the Creator - lessons that draw Susan and Eric closer to God.

Then one day, an encounter with a monster of the deep thrusts Eric face to face with his deepest fears - and puts his faith to the test. Will Eric trust God to help him overcome his terror and keep him safe from harm?

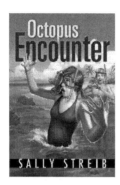

Octopus Encounter
Book 3

Suddenly, something red hurtled right at Susan. Splat! It hit her mask and hung on. She struggled to her feet, screaming to her brother and jumping about. "Get it off! Get it off!"

"It's an octopus!" Eric screamed.

Come along with Susan, Eric, Aunt Sally and Uncle Merle on another underwater adventure. This time they're in Cayman. Susan is trying to discover her individual talents, interests, and spiritual gifts.

Until recently, the twins had always done everything together. But now Eric is going in a new direction—following his passion for underwater photography. Working with Mr. Wood at the Scripps Institute, Eric has been busy sorting, identifying, and enhancing the underwater photos he took on the previous trip to Eleuthera Island.

Susan wishes she had something that could make her feel as excited as Eric seems to be. She tried joining Eric at the institute, but discovered that trying to be like her brother isn't the answer. She will have to find her own consuming passion. But what will it be?

Triton's Treasure

Steps to Christ for Kids

"The Triton Trumpet is one of your best creations," I whispered to God. "I just have to find a good specimen." When author Sally Streib whispered this short prayer, she could hardly imagine that one day she would posses one of the largest Triton Trumpet sea shells ever found and uncover its hidden message about forgiveness.

Discover how nature can bring you closer to your Creator. Triton's Treasure - Steps to Christ for Kids brings twenty new nature stories from author and storyteller Sally Streib.

In these stories, you will learn how you can walk closer with your Creator, Jesus Christ. Patterned after the best selling Steps to Christ, by Ellen G. White, Triton's Treasure shows the easy steps anyone can take to get to know Christ as a Friend and Savior.

"Look at the wonderful and beautiful things of nature...all speak to us of the Creator's love." Steps to Christ, Ellen G. White. With each new discovery, in and around the ocean, nature will reveal the truth about God and His love for you.